Turkish Diaries

A collection of short stories from my time living in Turkey

Matilda Voss

ALSO BY MATILDA VOSS

A Turkish Affair

Summer of Aydin ~ a short story

TURKISH DIARIES © 2019 MATILDA VOSS

'*Loving life is easy when you are abroad. Where no one knows you and you hold your life in your hands all alone, you are more master of yourself than at any other time.*'

Hannah Arendt

'*Ordinary life does not interest me.*'

Anais Nin

MATILDA VOSS

TURKISH DIARIES

CONTENTS

Introduction...1

Never a dull moment..5

How it all began..7

The challenges of flat hunting.....................................11

What's in the bag?...15

My weekly visit to the market......................................19

Tragedy on the Dardanelles...23

My cell phone debacle..28

Colour and curls calamity...32

Rubbish, rubbish everywhere......................................38

The long and the short of it 41

One scary night in Izmit..45

A dangerous collection..48

Earthquake...52

Priceless garden gnomes.. 55

Footprints on the wall...60

The big business of ANZAC Day.............................. 66

How to outsmart a greedy landlord.............................. 71

China products..76

Yabanci...79

Treasure..83

'This is Turkey'..87

I scream ice cream 91

'If you kill a cat...'...93

Dogs..96

Personal space..99

Excitement on the terraces..103

Anne's cooking..106

Thoughts on work..109

'The naked man'...112

Breakfast with Arzu...116

My postoffice meltdown..119

Facing my fears at the hamam..124

2009 Travels with my son..129

Room for two, please..131

Trapped...135

Seriously sick in Şanlıurfa 142

Abraham and his carp pool...146

The beehive houses of Harran..150

Sunset at Mount Nemrut..155

Welcome to Mardin...159

Keep Hasankeyf Alive..163

Our visit to the Diyarbakir Military Base.........................166

2010 – 2015 My solo travels.......................................171

Istanbul, Istanbul..173

The kindness of strangers...180

Paragliding off Babadağ 185

A Sunday feast out east...189

The best bus trip ever..194

My hitch-hiking adventures..201

Picnic at the lake..208

Balloons and fairy chimneys.......................................212

The creepiest musueum in the world................................216

2015 Time to move on..219

Leaving Turkey..221

Taking off my battle jacket.......................................226

Glossary..231

A Turkish Affair..233

About the author 235

Thank you...237

Introduction

In December of 2008, I made the massive life changing decision to leave Australia and move to Turkey to begin my new career as an English teacher.

It was an exciting time for me. The teaching position I had accepted was in an industrial city called Izmit, about an hour outside of Istanbul. It catered mostly to the engineering students from the local Kocaeli University.

It didn't take too long for me to develop a deep affection for my adopted country. I had eased into my new life there with no real difficulties. Of course, I had to navigate the usual issues such as the lack of the local language and finding a flat. Finding a hairdresser that spoke English was probably my biggest challenge at that time.

I loved my students. I loved the food. I embraced the culture.

I was hungry to learn as much as I could about everything Turkish. I read books written by Turkish authors such as Orhan Pamuk and Elif Shafak. I listened to Turkish music and filled my IPod with the sounds of Sezen Aksu, Tarkan, Mustafa Sandal and Teoman.

I felt that perhaps I had been a Turk or a Muslim in a previous life. Turkey just fitted me like a glove. I certainly was not religious in any way, but I loved waking to the *ezan*, the call to prayer. As it echoed from mosque to mosque, it reminded me constantly of where I was and how lucky I was to be living this life.

For anyone who has been to Turkey, perhaps they can understand how I felt. Turkey has a way of getting under your skin. In Turkey, my life was totally unpredictable and exciting. Everyday brought new experiences and challenges and I felt totally alive.

When I returned to Australia to visit family and friends, I could only rave on about my life in Turkey and how wonderful it was to live there. I was a huge ambassador for Turkey and encouraged my friends to holiday there.

Throughout the six and a half years that I lived there, I travelled extensively to every corner of this diverse country. In 2010, Istanbul was the European Capital of Culture. Turkey was at the top of the list of most desirable tourist destinations. Everyone wanted to come to Turkey and everyone left with colourful memories and experiences.

Now, sadly, due to terrorist attacks, a military coup, Russian relations and its questionable politics, Turkey is no longer the dream destination. Tourism has taken a severe hit.

I also no longer live in Turkey as it became apparent to me and many other expatiates around 2015/16 that it was time to leave. The

Turkey we had grown to love was changing and not in a good way.

Still, I look back at those years with so much fondness and still feel a strong connection. I actually miss the madness and the chaos, the delicious food, the simple moments of enjoying a Turkish coffee with friends in one of the cafes along the seafront.

What follows is a collection of short stories, anecdotes gathered from my life as an expatiate living in Turkey. They are all true stories and I think give an insight into Turkish life through the eyes of a foreigner. They illustrate the good, the bad and the ugly, the colour, the warmth of the locals and the unpredictability and randomness of everyday life.

Never a dull moment

my everyday life in Turkey

TURKISH DIARIES

How it all began

If you have read my previous book 'A Turkish Affair', you will have an idea of how my story evolved. An unhappy marriage and eventual divorce led me to seek a means of supporting my travel dreams. I completed a Teach English as a Foreign Language course, better know by its acronym of TEFL and then got my first teaching position in Izmit, Turkey.

It was certainly an exciting time for me. Anyone that's gone through divorce might understand that insatiable urge for adventure and freedom. The shackles were off and the world was beckoning.

I look back now and see how brave I was. I think I was so desperate to experience the world that I didn't even consider the risks. I didn't waste any energy on thinking about what hardships I might experience or anything negative. I wanted to feel alive and anyway, what's the worst thing that could happen? I had organized a job, I had some money and worse comes to worse, I could always return home.

So I packed my suitcase and flew to Turkey. It was that simple. I couldn't have chosen a better country to start this new chapter of my life. English teaching was a rewarding experience and I got to travel all over this amazing nation.

I hot air ballooned in Cappadocia. I para-glided from Babadağ, a mountain 2000 metres above sea level near Fethiye. I attended an ANZAC Day dawn ceremony at Gallipoli, a significant day in Australia's history. I visited so many amazing archaeological sites such as Ephesus and Pergamon. I actually lived a stone's throw away from the renowned city of Troy made famous by Homer's Iliad. I even got to meet Bo Derek after she swam the historic Hellespont Swim Race, four and a half kilometres across the Dardanelles from Europe to Asia.

My first lesson teaching English in Izmit was terrifying. I think back now and laugh as I recall how nervous I was. I did get a lot of support but my inexperience made me self conscious. It took a few weeks until I actually started to feel confident. I always did a lot of preparation for my classes because even though one is a native English speaker, sometimes explaining grammar points is a challenge. To feel confident, I needed to feel prepared.

At my school, lessons were in the morning from 10 am till 2 pm and then in the evening from 6 pm to 10 pm. I really enjoyed the evening classes more. There was a different energy in the classroom, more informal perhaps.

I have some wonderful memories from those days. I found my students to be at all times, respectful and generous. They would refer to me as 'my teacher' and often after class they would be eager for me to meet their mothers, grandmothers or any other family member. On many occasions, I was delighted to receive gifts of home-made baklava or dolma, the stuffed grape leaves. Once I was given a tube of foot cream which did seem strange but as the sentiment goes, 'its the thought that counts.' I might add that my email address at the time was 'itchyfeet' and perhaps this was the reason.

One Mother's Day, I arrived at school to be showered with flowers. I guess that was because they knew that my children were in Australia. They wished to comfort me with flowers. It was such a beautiful gesture but slightly embarrassing as none of the other teachers received flowers. I was touched by their thoughtfulness and kindness.

Some classes were unforgettable as my students would love to show me their musical talents. They would bring their instruments to class, be it a Turkish flute called a *ney* or the *saz*, a type of long necked lute that plays the wonderfully soulful sounds of Turkish folk music. How honoured I would feel. Another memorable class was when a few of my students had practiced a traditional folk dance routine to perform for me. Certainly, as much as I was teaching these students English, they were giving me so much more.

Teaching in Izmit had been a rewarding opportunity and it had confirmed that I had made the right decision to follow this new career path. The students in Izmit were mostly engineering students from the nearby Kocaeli university.

A year later I accepted a teaching position in Çanakkale, a city on the Dardanelles and near the ancient city of Troy. Here, my students were mostly from the University of Çanakkale or *Onsekiz Mart* University as its known. *Onsekiz Mart* refers to the date 18 March, 1915 when the Turkish successfully repelled the British and French forces during World War One.

Generally speaking, I found the students here not to be as enthusiastic about learning English. They were constantly late to class and often would not participate but preferred to play on their phones. Despite low scores in exams, all students passed. It was all about the money and ensuring that they signed up for the next course. Such a difference from my school in Izmit.

I also had the challenge of teaching children during the summer months. The students in these classes ranged from 6 to 16 years old. I really earned my money teaching those classes as most of the children didn't want to be there. Games got out of hand, the boys liked to rough and tumble and the few girls that did attend were so outnumbered that they couldn't be heard. The end of summer couldn't come quick enough.

As in Izmit, life in Çanakkale was never a dull moment. I moved flats numerous times, was homeless for a few weeks, experienced my first serious earthquake, enjoyed the numerous parades and celebrations, experienced snowy winter days, whirling dervish concerts, Sezen Aksu in the streets, the Troya Festival, Gallipoli and Anzac Day, saw Julia Gillard, the Australian Prime Minister at the time, give a moving speech to the attendees.

I loved the impressive history of Çanakkale and the knowledge that I was walking where Alexander the Great had passed thousands of years before and where Xerxes had built his bridge of boats to cross the Dardanelles. To see the actual city of Troy was amazing, a topic that I had studied in ancient history class at high school. Yes, I loved my life in Çanakkale and ended up staying there for over five years.

Everything was good, really good until it wasn't.

The challenges of flat hunting

As the *emlak* opened the door to the apartment building, an offensive smell assaulted our senses.

Janet had been kind enough to accompany me on my flat hunting expedition. She had lived in Çanakkale for over ten years and her Turkish was fluent whereas mine was very basic.

On moving to Çanakkale to teach English in 2010, my first flat had been provided by my school and had been very comfortable. I could even go so far as to say that I had been very happy there. It was on the top floor of the academy building and had a lovely terrace where I could sit and read and enjoy the sunshine. It even had a bit of a sea view between the large hotels that surrounded me. I'd lived there in complete ex-pat bliss for fourteen months but then, unfortunately, my manager was taken seriously ill and forced to sell his school and building and I was suddenly homeless.

At the time, the building boom that is apparent today hadn't started in Çanakkale and it was becoming a stress that I couldn't find a new home. I had easily found a new teaching job but the flat situation was dire. I was drifting between friends' sofas and hotels.

In Turkey, the real estate agents are called *emlaks*. There are *emlak* offices on every corner as in Turkey, anyone can be an *emlak* and their reputation isn't the best. All around the world, the reputation of a real estate agent can be somewhat like that of a second hand car dealer; unscrupulous, dishonest and out to cheat the customer in every way possible. Of course, not all are this way, and I do apologize to the honest ones. However in Turkey, *emlaks* take it up a notch and are a force to be feared.

In my quest to find a new home, the *emlaks* had a field day with me. They would sit behind their desk, smoking and drinking *çay*, whilst checking me out and calculating how much they could get out of me. They always wanted a full week's rent as a searcher's fee. One very sleazy *emlak* always offered me wine and made me feel very uncomfortable whilst I sat waiting for him to search through his listings.

Despite clearly explaining my needs, I had been shown flats that were actually office space with no bathroom or kitchen. I was taken to see a flat below a house that had a dirt floor. One flat was quite reasonable except for the fact that I was expected to buy and install the hot water system. Another flat that I had spotted from the road and ventured up to see had no windows in the bedroom and bathroom. Then there were the many flats in the most unimaginable states of filth.

As we entered the foyer and began to slowly ascend the stairs to the fourth floor the smell was getting stronger.

"What is that dreadful smell?" I inquired.

Janet and I were both pinching our noses but the *emlak* didn't seem to notice.

"Nothing," he said. "The cleaner will come next week."

The smell was suffocating and both Janet and I were green. All of a sudden it came to me what the disgusting odour was.

"It smells like dog," I exclaimed.

"No, no," replied the *emlak*.

Janet had come to the same conclusion. It was definitely the stench of enclosed dogs. As we continued up the final flight of stairs, the *emlak* still insisted that there were no dogs in the building.

He put the key into the door and as he opened the door to the flat I half expected a dog to run at us but there was no dog in sight. The smell, however, was overbearing.

The *emlak* happily showed me the kitchen and opened all the cupboards to show me the crockery and cutlery that was available for my use. He proceeded to the bathroom and the balcony. Whilst it wasn't an old flat and did have some possibilities, I had already dismissed it as an option due to the heavy pong which the *emlak* still insisted wasn't from a dog.

There were two bedrooms but one of the doors was closed. I opened the door and was about to step inside when the startled beast sprang into action, pulling aggressively on his chain with eyes filled with hate. He lunged at me and of course, I screamed. It became apparent that I had just woken up a sleeping Rottweiler and he wasn't happy. Drool dripped from his mouth as he fiercely bared his teeth, pulling at his chain. I fell back against Janet in fear and disbelief. The *emlak* just stood there.

The poor Rottweiler had been chained to the bed on which he had been sleeping. Despite my initial horror, I now felt a sense of pity and pain for this poor creature. God knows how long he had been imprisoned up there. This was, after all, a blatant case of cruelty to animals and sadly it wasn't the first time I had witnessed such abuse of dogs in Turkey.

I looked at the *emlak* in disgust. Janet and I were sickened beyond words.

"If you want the flat, the dog will be out by the end of the month," he said.

What's in the bag?

"Why are you carrying that heavy looking bag around?" I asked.

My friend Aysel had introduced me online to a colleague of her husband. They were both in the military together and based near Izmir.

The nature of their work was highly confidential and even Aysel didn't know the details of the special ops her husband was involved in. She could tell me that Ramazan was divorced, had a teenage daughter and spoke perfect English. According to her, he was very fit, handsome and desperately wanted to meet someone.

We had chatted a few times on Skype and there had seemed to be some chemistry. He was interesting and colourful. He shared stories of his time spent training in the United States where he had also perfected his English. He had served in many hotspots around the globe including Serbia, Iraq and somewhere in Africa. He had been a paratrooper and had just recently done a parachuting refresher course. I was fascinated and we were both ready to meet in person.

With my work, I didn't have time to travel all the way to Izmir and I didn't really want him to come to Çanakkale either. We both thought it was best to meet for the first time somewhere impartial, somewhere not too far to travel. We both agreed Ayvalik was an excellent compromise; halfway between our cities, an attractive seaside town with a distinctly Greek flavour and many fine seafood restaurants. It would be the perfect place to enjoy some fine wine and the delicious Turkish cuisine whilst getting to know each other and watching the sun set over the Aegean.

He met me at the Ayvalik bus station and we then drove down to Cunda Island or Alibey Adasi in Turkish, where we would enjoy the evening. Though an island, Cunda is connected to Ayvalik by a long causeway and is the resort area of Ayvalik, a collection of romantic boutique hotels and quaint cobbled streets and lanes.

It was early afternoon and we agreed on a spot of lunch. Ramazan parked the car. I was, of course, content to leave my small bag in the boot of his car but Ramazan proceeded to take his big black bag out of the car and bring it with us. I didn't comment but I did wonder.

"Is it safe for me to leave my bag in the car here?" I asked.

"Yes, of course," he replied.

I was naturally perplexed as to why it was safe to leave my bag in the car and yet he had to bring his.

We entered a cozy courtyard of a small café and took our seats surrounded by garden. Ramazan placed his bag at his feet and we ordered some lunch. Our conversation flowed and I was quite comfortable being with Ramazan.

After lunch we walked along the seafront enjoying the fresh air and taking in our wonderful surroundings. All the time, Ramazan carried his bag around with him.

"Why don't you put it in the car," I suggested. "It looks quite heavy."

"It's OK," he replied.

I didn't want to harp on the matter but it did seem strange.

We eventually found our hotel and decided to have a short rest, freshen up and meet down in the foyer at seven.

Ramazan suggested a scenic drive around Ayvalik before dinner and of course, the black bag accompanied us. When we got out of the car to explore the beach, the black bag came too. I was intrigued. What could possibly be in that bag that was so important or valuable that he couldn't leave it in the car or in his hotel room?

Eventually, we drove back to Cunda Island to go for dinner in one of the picturesque seafront restaurants. So far the day had been most enjoyable with excellent conversation in a beautiful and romantic setting. Just the bag baffled me. I was mystified, bewildered, perplexed. He seemed a normal enough guy but his attachment to his bag just didn't make sense.

We parked the car and Ramazan proceeded to retrieve his bag from the back seat. It was now going to accompany us to dinner.

"Seriously Ramazan, what is in that bag?" I blurted out.

It had become so frustrating that I just had to know. I couldn't think about anything else. Perhaps he had a huge stash of money? Gold? What could it possibly be?

Ramazan stared at me deeply. He looked around at our immediate environment. He motioned me over to his side of the car. He placed the bag on the driver's seat. Still looking around in every direction and checking our privacy, he motioned me closer. I was bursting with anticipation.

Slowly and cautiously he began to unzip the big black bag. I watched intently as every centimetre of the zip gave way to expose the contents. I was gobsmacked. I don't know what I was expecting but it certainly wasn't that; an arsenal of weapons.

I had never been that close to a gun in my life and now I was staring down at a bag full of serious looking weaponry. Looking me seriously in the eye, Ramazan quickly zipped the bag back up and swung it over his shoulder and we headed over to the restaurant.

No more was said about the big black bag that continued to accompany us on our weekend getaway. Thankfully, he didn't need to open it again.

My weekly visit to the market

He saw me checking out his produce and beckoned me over; a large stout fellow with a shiny face, a big smile and a really filthy apron.

"*Buyrun*," he called, welcoming me to his stall.

I walked over to closer examine his *incir* or dried figs. Twelve lira a kilo seemed very reasonable. The sign said that they were from the southern province of Aydin. On a previous trip down south I had seen how these figs were dried in the sun and packaged for sale and even for export to countries as far away as Australia. The memory of all the flies crawling all over them always made me cringe but I guess it was at least a natural process and I hadn't heard of anyone dying from eating dried figs. I did love figs.

Seeing my interest and, keen to seal the deal, he carefully selected one fig from the juicy pile and began to gently massage it between his thick grubby fingers. Using his thumbs, he then prized it open and placed a hazel nut inside and moulded it back together. With a radiant smile and an outstretched hand, he gestured for me to come closer and accept his offering.

"Hmm, what should I do," I thought to myself.

I certainly didn't want to offend but on the other hand, the vision of his grubby fingers was etched in my mind.

"*Teşekkür ederim,*" I thanked him.

I couldn't refuse his generosity and so I graciously took the fig from his hand and popped into my mouth. I tried not to think about the state of his fingers and where they may have been.

The fig was delicious and I did buy a kilo of his succulent figs and of course, some hazelnuts. What a clever salesman he was.

My weekly trips to the local fruit and vegetable market were always an enjoyable adventure for me. I had never seen such an abundance of deliciously fresh produce. Vegetables were piled high and inviting me to buy them. I could never resist and always took home way to much for the week. I eventually had to do as the locals do and buy myself a shopping cart to carry all my purchases home. I loved the colour and the energy of the market. I often took my camera as there were brilliant photo opportunities down every lane.

There was the robust village lady with whiskers and a headscarf, wearing her big baggy *şalvar,* walking around whilst carrying a few live chickens by their feet. She would call out her price and eager customers would flock to her to inspect the chickens.

There was the gaggle of village ladies sitting crosslegged on the ground selling their herbs and partaking in a spot of local gossip. The activity at the different stalls never ceased. The vendors were constantly stacking and positioning their produce, shining them up, spraying them with water and calling out their special offers.

"*Patates, bir buçuk lira*", he called.

Potatoes, one and a half lira a kilogram.

Everything was sold by the kilogram and they didn't waste their time selling you a couple of tomatoes. They would just give them to you. And so I learnt to buy all my supplies by the kilogram which, of course, was too much for me. However, it did encourage me to eat more vegetables and that can only be good.

At the markets you could buy just about anything you needed but I generally stuck to the fresh produce area. As well as my fruit and vegetable supplies, I also bought my white cheese, hard cheese, olives, fresh honey, fresh honey comb, nuts, dried fruits and eggs there.

Occasionally, I would wander to the front section of the market where the stalls sold an assortment of household goods like pots and pans, brooms and brushes, tools and linen as well as clothing, shoes and bags. There were a couple of vendors that sold underwear and it was funny to see bras of every size and colour hanging on display above their table.

One time I needed to buy a new towel and wandered over to the linen section. The man was standing up on a chair and calling out his special offers. There was a mountain of towels, all sizes and colours, thrown on the table and women were aggressively sorting, pulling and pushing. I spied a large turquoise towel that I wanted but how could I reach it? I would try to battle my way through the throng of eager shoppers, my arm outstretched to try and reach it.

"When in Rome, do as the Romans do." Well, I was trying my best to act like a Turkish woman and grab for the towel I wanted. The vendor, who was enjoying all the crazy drama at his table and his wife collecting all the lira, had spotted me and obviously saw that I was not a local. He pointed at the different towels until he reached the one I wanted and grabbed it from the pile and threw it in a bag for me and that was it. I handed over my ten lira and proudly took home my extra large turquoise bath towel.

A simple pleasure, but visiting the market was always a highlight of my week and something I really miss now since moving away.

Tragedy on the Dardanelles

"What was that?"

I heard it clearly. A loud splash followed by lots of confused chatter. Everyone had heard it but no one had seen anything.

I was returning from my trip to Spain and after a four and a half hour flight to Istanbul, I then needed to take the six and a half hour bus to my home in Çanakkale. Luckily, the buses run from Istanbul to Çanakkale every hour and so I rarely had to wait long to catch one. The buses are very comfortable with refreshments served along the way but still the trip is long and tiresome. It is a three-hundred-and- twenty kilometre journey but the bus stops at every town along the way plus there is a thirty-minute break at a roadside café and then at the end there is the twenty-five minute Dardanelles crossing by ferry. It's tedious.

I love to travel abroad but after a few years of living in Çanakkale, I always dreaded this bus trip home. This particular night

I had estimated that I would be home by around two in the morning. I was already exhausted from my travels around Spain and I just longed for my bed. Travel is awesome but so is coming home.

The bus wasn't that full and being evening, everyone was quite content to relax and watch a program on the screens on the back of the seats. I was lucky enough to have a free seat next to me so I could spread out a little and maybe even dose off a little.

I noticed that the lady behind me also had a free seat next to her and had her bags on it. I had noticed that, even though she wore the headscarf, she was dressed quite modern and was perhaps somewhere in her forties. I had smiled at her as I took my seat and she had smiled back. A small exchange of pleasantries and I only wish we had exchanged more.

In general, bus travel in Turkey is probably the best I've ever experienced. All the buses are modern and the ticket prices are extremely good value. I usually enjoy bus travel except for this trip because I had done it so many times and knew every twist and turn on the road and every town that we stopped at.

During the summertime, the buses were always completely full and I didn't enjoy those trips. On one particular trip during the summer months, I was heading down to Izmir and I took my seat on the aisle, only to have a rather large woman and her child who I would have guessed to be nine or ten years old, motion to me that they were in the window seat. It is a common occurrence that people don't want to pay for their children to travel and hence buy only one ticket and have the child on their lap or standing by the window. I guess they hope that there will be some free seats but as this wasn't the case, I had to endure the discomfort of this duo next to me. But travelling in the off-season, I usually managed to get a seat all to myself and the trip was usually pleasant and peaceful.

Also on the buses, it's forbidden for a woman to sit next to a man unless they are related, so men often have a free seat next to them, whilst us woman are all bundled together. Once I asked for a ticket and was told that the bus was fully booked. I asked another desk if there were any free seats and was told that the only free seat was next to a man. I said that I didn't mind sitting next to a man and it was not a problem for me, but they insisted that it was against regulations and so I had to wait for the next bus.

This night, the trip home was going smoothly. I didn't sleep at all but relaxed with my music and thought about my bed awaiting me at home. I would sleep in and then meet my friend for a late breakfast at one of the cafes along the seafront. I had been away for three weeks and so the thought of home was overwhelming.

The bus followed its usual route out through Silivri stopping at Tekirdağ, and then every little town along the way until I am happy to see the sign for Gelibolu and know that we are getting close now. The next stop is Eceabat and the car ferry.

As the bus pulls into Eceabat, I am only a stone's throw from home. Well, not really. It's about a twenty five minute ferry boat ride across the Dardanelles. We are on the northern side of the Dardanelles which is still classified as Europe and we will cross the four or five kilometres over to the Asian side or Anatolia as it's known. That last part of the trip always seems to take forever. The ferries are quite frequent but they travel very slowly. In summer it's a nightmare as the volume of cars makes it a much longer wait.

This night we are lucky and our bus rolls straight onto the waiting ferryboat and takes its position at the front. Many passengers take this opportunity to have a stroll around the ferry, get some fresh air and gaze across at the brilliantly lit vista that is Çanakkale. The ferryboats also have a café aboard and many passengers enjoy a cigarette and something to eat or drink.

I had decided to stay on the bus, comfortable and warm in my seat, and just wait for my arrival home. From the ferry port it was only a ten minute walk to my flat but I had already decided that I would take a taxi this evening. It was late and I was exhausted.

I could hear the massive motor of the ferryboat starting to churn and could feel that we were slowly pulling out from the Eceabat harbour. Soon I would be home. It had been a very long day and it was now two o'clock in the morning.

Even though I stayed on the bus, I clearly heard the loud splash. I heard some passengers gasping and then the chatter about what had happened. No one was really sure. Someone thought that they had seen a woman jump into the sea. The ferry boat was brought to a sudden halt. Passengers lined the railings. Everyone was searching the surrounding waters for what was now confirmed to be a woman who had jumped from the deck.

The Çanakkale Coast Guard soon arrived and lit up the otherwise dark waters with their brilliant lights. It was a cold, dark night. There was no moon to help the search. I soon realized that the woman in the seat behind mine had gone and she had left many packages on her seat. Was she out searching the waters from the deck or was she the victim?

It was well over an hour later that the search was called off. Our ferryboat and the two coast guard boats had circled the sea but no body was found. Everyone had been loaded back onto their buses to gather their belongings for our arrival in Çanakkale. The woman in the seat behind me never returned to take her bags and packages.

The next day I related my story to my friend but it was another day later that her body was washed ashore on the northern side of the Dardanelles at a town called Kilitbahir, about six kilometres from Eceabat.

The newspaper ran the story that she had left packages for her family and a long letter for her sister. She had been abused by her husband and had tried many times to leave him but he always found her. The abuse continued. She could see no way out but to take her own life.

The abuse of women by their husbands and the lack of women's rights in general, was one of the reasons for my decision to leave Turkey after six and a half years. Domestic violence was noticeably on the increase with a staggering four-hundred-and thirteen murders of women reported by media in 2015 and the numbers increasing in 2016. There was also a noticeable rise in female suicides. It was just too hard to turn a blind eye to those shocking statistics.

My cell phone debacle

It was time; time to upgrade to a Smart phone.

When I first moved to Turkey to teach English in Izmit, my school had helped me to buy a cell phone with a Turkish SIM card. Naturally, I chose the cheapest Nokia as I didn't think I was going to still be in Turkey by the end of the year.

It was a couple of years later and to everyone's surprise, including me, I was still in Turkey; still teaching English and still enjoying the life in my adopted country. By now, my cell phone just wasn't serving my needs. I needed to be able to go online. I needed a smartphone and I had my eye on a mid-range, medium priced Samsung.

I had been researching and checking prices and had finally decided to go in and make the purchase. As is usual in Turkey, the shop assistants are always eager to serve. He wanted to show me some different, more expensive models but I knew which one I wanted. I pointed it out in the display cabinet and it was an easy sale for him.

He disappeared to the back of the shop for a moment and came back with the Samsung box and opened it to show me the phone inside. It was the correct model but something bothered me. I queried him as to why the box wasn't enclosed in cellophane. He assured me that it had been and that he had just now taken the plastic off. He saw the doubt on my face and further assured me that it was a brand new phone. Of course, I had to believe him but I still had this niggling feeling in the pit of my stomach that something wasn't right.

Totally ignoring my intuition, I paid the man in cash and happily took my new phone home, excited to set it up and install the apps that I wanted. The world of apps had exploded and I was thrilled to be finally able to join in on all the fun.

When I arrived home, my friend dropped by for coffee. Naturally, I was keen to show off my new phone. I let him check it out whilst I made coffee.

"Who's the guy in the photo?

"What guy?" I asked. "I just bought it. I haven't used it yet."

He clarified, "There is a picture of a guy on your phone. Who is he?"

"I don't know what you are talking about," I exclaimed.

I really had no idea what he was on about. I hadn't taken any photos. I had just bought the phone half an hour earlier.

"Let me see," I asked.

He was right. There was a picture of a Turkish man, maybe in his thirties, on my 'new' phone.

"Well, I swear I didn't take that photo. I don't know who it is. How could it be on my phone?"

My friend was just laughing now. I didn't see the joke.

"You've been had," he explained.

"How?" I cried.

"Obviously, this isn't a new phone and I'm guessing you paid for a new phone."

I then remembered how the box had been missing the cellophane seal and how the assistant had told me that he had just then removed it. Why hadn't I insisted on a sealed box? Why hadn't I followed my gut instinct? When was I going to learn? This certainly wasn't the first time that I had been duped whilst living in Turkey.

In fact, only the previous week, I had gone into a similar shop to ask for a phone battery for my friend's mother.

"Ask for the Chinese product," he had told me. "It's much cheaper."

I had forgotten and just asked for a phone battery with the model number. The guy gave me the battery and quoted his price. It seemed a little steep. Then I remembered about the Chinese product.

"Oh, can I have the Chinese product, please?"

The guy looked at me strangely, turned around, pretended to change the battery but gave me the exact same one and with a smile asked me for half the amount he had first quoted.

I really need to be less trusting, I thought.

Me, being a foreigner, *yabanci*, and a woman at that.....these guys saw the perfect opportunity to scam me. Well, this guy wasn't going to get away with it. I was livid. I was really getting tired of always paying double or being short changed just because I was a foreigner. It was something one has to get used to when you live in Turkey but it always made me feel so hurt and stupid.

I couldn't sit down and relax. I needed to get back down to the store and demand a new phone or my money back. I had been living in Turkey long enough to know that I needed a plan of action, some sort of threat or something that would ensure that I would get satisfaction. I could threaten to get the police but everybody knows that the police aren't going to respond to a petty crime such as this.

I googled the shop's name and found the phone number and name of the proprietor. It was actually a small chain of stores. I thought that just the name of the proprietor was probably enough at this stage.

I stormed into the shop and asked to speak to the store manager. I needed to look strong. I explained my concerns and demands and showed the manager the picture on my phone. I explained that I had spoken to the owner in Istanbul and he had told me to return to the store and ask for new phone.

If I was refused, I was to call him again. He also said that if the matter wasn't resolved, the assistant that sold me the used phone would be dismissed immediately.

In Turkey, jobs are hard to find and a job in a phone shop is considered a decent one, so I knew that this threat wouldn't be taken lightly. I just wanted a new phone.

The manager promptly took my phone and handed me a new box completely enclosed in cellophane and apologized for this incident. It was that simple.

I felt like I had won a major victory. I had been cheated and tricked many times, so it felt good to finally win one. It was another lesson learned; to always follow my gut and to always be vigilant. Not a great way to live, I agree, but just a fact of life in Turkey.

Colour and curls calamity

As I previously mentioned, one of the biggest stresses I faced during my time in Turkey was going to the hairdressers. This simple act which was mostly enjoyable back home in Australia caused me so much anxiety and fear here in Turkey. Why, you ask?

Well, for a start, the language barrier. I didn't speak very much Turkish and I couldn't find a hair dresser that spoke any English. You might suggest that I take a friend or student to translate for me. That sounds perfectly reasonable. What about taking a photograph along? That's also a perfectly reasonable idea. Well, it isn't. Nothing was. It just never worked out. What I wanted and what they thought I should have were two very different ideas. There were my wishes and then there were the ideas of the hairdresser and then to totally add to the disaster, the ideas of my translators.

It was a constant nightmare and the time of the month that I really dreaded and feared. I guess it sounds really petty, but just try and imagine my situation.

I have curly light brown hair. It's the kind of hair that needs a regular cut or else it gets so unruly and bushy. Also, as I'm of that age when gray hairs are appearing, I do like to get a colour as well, just a subtle tint, nothing extreme. As I said, back home I always enjoyed the experience. I'd sit back with a coffee in a massage chair and simply relax with my favourite gossip magazine for an hour or so.

In Turkey my early experiences were a nightmare. I asked for recommendations and I also scoured the neighbourhood looking for fresh modern looking salons. I settled on one. Its name was 'Angels' if I remember correctly. I took along a Turkish teacher from my school who gave English lessons and her level of English was quite good, I thought. Still, somehow things got terribly lost in translation.

The salon was upstairs in an old building but it was accessible by elevator. On entering I was pleasantly surprised as it looked very efficient and well organized. I was greeted as a celebrity as my colleague announced that I was from Australia. The manager and a small group of stylists encircled me, smiling, welcoming me, and touching my hair. I felt insecure and didn't enjoy the attention but I had to be strong.

My colleague explained that I'd like a colour first and that I usually used L'Oréal. They didn't have L'Oréal and proceeded to show me the book of samples. After some discussion with my colleague, I chose the colour that I wanted and she forwarded my request. She had offered her opinion that I should go for a darker colour but I was happy to go with my selection as it was close to my present hair colour. I had never been adventurous in the hair department and liked to stay with my natural colour and just cover up the few grays.

I watched on as she and the hairdresser, a man, discussed my colour, always turning and sending me brief glances. I felt like my life was in their hands. Finally, they approached me, led me to a chair and covered me with a robe. He went away, I presumed to concoct my colour.

After over six years living in Turkey, I have realized that I have never had a female hairdresser. Strangely they are all males, with the female staff only washing and blow drying.

Anyway, back to this hellish experience. He soon reappeared with a bowl in hand and began to apply my colour, all the while, at least three assistants and my colleague looking on. I felt like I was the morning's entertainment. I can't say I was feeling at all confident but I tried to smile and act normal.

The hairdresser was applying the colour around my hairline and combing through my roots.

"That looks darker than normal," I nervously commented.

"No, no. It's just while it's wet," my colleague replied.

"Are you sure?" I queried.

A short discussion began between her and the hairdresser. The rest of the crew eagerly watched on.

"OK, he says it's a little bit darker than what you chose but he assures me you will like it," she replied.

"What? Why?"

I was really not happy.

"He thinks it will look better and the colour will last longer," she replied nervously.

"I can't believe this," I answered her angrily.

I was fuming. I was anxious. I just wanted to be out of there.

"Just relax. It will be fine," she tried to calm me.

I had to go through the process and wait for what I knew was going to be a disaster.

Waiting and watching as the colour just seemed to get darker and darker.

Finally, it was time to rinse out the colour and see the results.

"Oh my God, that's terrible," I exclaimed as I looked at my extremely dark brown hair in the mirror.

"No, you look beautiful," replied my colleague with the small gathering all agreeing.

"Can we make it lighter?" I exploded.

"Why? It's so beautiful."

I'd had enough. There was no way I was letting this guy come at me with scissors.

"This isn't what I asked for and it isn't the colour I chose," I exclaimed.

"But the hairdresser recommends this colour for you," my colleague, soon to be ex-friend, declared.

"I want to leave now."

"OK, OK. But first he wants to dry your hair properly. Are you sure you don't want him to cut it?" she asked.

"No, definitely not." I was seething with anger.

Next, he took to me with the blow-dryer; all the while one of his girls was dutifully holding the apparatus and handing it to him when he requested it. Again, I tried to explain that I was naturally curly and so I liked it rather natural looking and just a bit of drying off would be fine.

On went a giant dollop of some sticky foamy product and away he went, moving his body in rhythm as he blow dried my hair, again not listening to anything I had said. He even took out his comb and did a little tease, all the time acting like he was on a stage doing the performance of his life.

"Beautiful," he exclaimed.

Everyone was watching on now as the maestro did his magic and I was the centre of attention, something I'm really not comfortable with. I just wanted to shrink away into the floor. By this stage I just wanted out. I had realized that it wasn't about what I wanted and never would be and so it was easiest to accept defeat and get out of there.

His masterpiece complete, I then had to face the further humiliation of a photo shoot with him and all his staff. My colleague was just looking on and smiling proudly. Everyone was quite pleased with themselves whilst I was ready to internally combust. I could feel the heat rising to my cheeks and a wave of nausea swept through my body.

I didn't want to make a scene and just paid the guy, grabbed my jacket and left as swiftly as I could. My colleague, who was running after me, continued to remark on how beautiful I looked. I was traumatized. I had gone in with light brown naturally curly hair and came out with a very dark brown Afro looking hair style somewhat like Michael Jackson in the early years.

All I could do was to get home as fast I could, wash out all the product and shampoo and shampoo endlessly to try and reduce the colour but to no avail. It was every woman's worst hair-do disaster. It was the hair-do from hell and I still needed to get it cut. It took over a month for the colour to fade slightly and for me to pluck up the courage to try once again.

I can say that it took a couple of years till I found a hairdresser that I could trust. Well, almost trust. There were other disasters of course, but perhaps I just got more used to it.

On a side note, one hairdressing salon that I was recommended to in Istanbul was called 'Violent Hair'.

"Violent?" I exclaimed. "What sort of hair dresser is that?"

I tried to explain that 'violent' wasn't a good name for a hairdresser as it conjured up all sorts of images of horror, much worse than just a bad cut and colour.

"In Turkey, a violent is a purple flower," I was told.

You can imagine my amusement.

"You mean violet. That's a purple flower," I laughed. "Violent means aggressive and fierce."

You would imagine that if they are going to use an English word that they would first check the spelling and the meaning, but that's Turkey, always full of surprises.

Rubbish, rubbish everywhere

There is no denying that Turkey is an amazingly beautiful country. How often was I awestruck by a stunning vista before me? I was lucky in that I got to see many different parts of the country and have travelled the length and breadth from border to border. My favourite place will always be Cappadocia, but then again I love Kaş and Olympia. Oh and the islands; Bozcaada and Gökçeada.

Living in Çanakkale, we were surrounded by beauty. Summer months were always spent at the Saros Gulf, located on the northern side of the Gallipoli Peninsula. The water was crystal clear and most of the time we had the beach all to ourselves. Tourists didn't venture past the Gallipoli Memorial at Anzac Cove and so generally, we only saw the odd fisherman or goat herder. In fact, a good friend of ours had a small fishing shack there where we often spent our summer weekends.

It was a small shed built from corrugated iron and timber, illegally of course, but inside it was comfortably set up to accommodate us for a relaxing and peaceful weekend. We loved going there. It could have been paradise but for one thing; the rubbish. It was like a rubbish dump.

Other visitors to the shack would make a bonfire and BBQ as would we, but they would throw the beer bottles, plastic bags, paper plates and cups, cigarette packets, wine bottles, plastic water bottles, foam food containers and whatever else all around the site. It was horrible. It was unbelievable. It was something I just couldn't comprehend. We would usually do a clean-up and then the next weekend when we visited it was the same.

As the summer progressed, the rubbish simply piled up. Disposable nappies could be found under every bush and all sorts of coloured plastics speckled the sand dunes. It was just horrendous and certainly tainted our little patch of paradise on the Gallipoli peninsula.

But this wasn't an isolated occurrence. Wherever I travelled in Turkey, sadly it was the same story. People would drive out to the countryside to throw their rubbish under the bushes, down a ravine or into a lake. On one occasion, I was traveling by bus with my eldest son and his girlfriend from the Pamukkale to Fethiye on the Mediterranean coast. They were visiting from Australia and we were doing an explore by bus to the southern regions.

Turkish buses are very comfortable and refreshments are usually served. On this particular bus trip, the service attendant had served us tea and coffee and a snack and was now in the process of cleaning up. He walked down the aisle collecting our papers and cups into a large plastic bag. We had been speeding along through some stunning countryside, with snow-capped mountains in the distance, when the bus suddenly slowed down and came to a complete stop in the middle of nowhere. The back door opened and to our shock and horror, the attendant climbed down the steps and threw the large bag of rubbish out into the bushes. We gasped and let him know our disgust at his action, but he just sent a wicked smile our way.

Back home in Çanakkale, I often took the local ferryboat which crossed the Dardanelles and connected the European side of Turkey to the Anatolian side. Here again, food and beverages are served on board and I can't count how many times I saw the passengers just throw their papers and bottles into the sea. I always made a point of telling the people that it was shameful behaviour but they just didn't see it. To them it was just normal. Throwing cigarette butts into the street or into the sea doesn't bat an eyelash.

I've been told by litterers that by throwing their rubbish into the streets it provides jobs for the street cleaners. This is a lame excuse that doesn't explain the rubbish being thrown into the forests, beaches and waterways.

Obviously, education about littering and polluting their environment has to start at school with the children but as yet this hasn't happened and sadly many beautiful places in Turkey are marred by piles of unsightly rubbish. Looking back at some photos I took at the ancient city of Harran on the Syrian border back in 2010, I noticed that every photo had coloured plastics in the foreground or background.

I would often to talk to my Turkish friends about this and they would agree that it was a problem but would then flick their cigarette onto the footpath. What a shame.

I am hopeful that in the near future, the Turkish people, who are fiercely patriotic and love their country, will see the damage that they are doing to their wonderful natural environment and just learn to pop their rubbish into the bin.

The long and the short of it

When one lives in Turkey, it's not long before you will become the victim of some kind of con or scam. Hopefully, it will only be a few lira here and there and nothing too traumatic. Being a foreigner, *yabanci*, it is widely assumed that you are wealthy and therefore the perfect candidate for overcharging and cheating. It's shocking and can be so frustrating. You need to have your wits about you at all times.

For tourists, a visit to the Istanbul's Grand Bazaar, *Kapalıçarşı,* is an adventure that requires you to be fully alert. Comments from the vendors such as, "Let me take your money, let me help you spend your money, let me help you buy things you don't need," all add to the Grand Bazaar experience. Those comments sound amusing but often that's exactly what happens. Then there are also all the fake products, fake brands, fake Turkish carpets which are mass-produced in China and of course, gross overcharging.

Add to that, the unscrupulous taxi drivers and it's almost impossible for tourists to avoid being scammed in some way or other. That's the short of it; small simple everyday cons that catch us by surprise and are difficult to avoid.

But for foreigners living in Turkey, they soon become aware of the more lengthy well thought-out scams that cost so much more, in some cases thousands and thousands of dollars. Yes, sadly that is one of the truths and realities about living in Turkey.

The long scams that I am referring to are when the perpetrator is prepared to invest months or even years into developing a relationship of trust with a foreigner. Then, when the friendship seems solid and honest, and the foreigner least expects it, the culprit will make his or her move. It could be for money or it could be for a foreign passport and a chance to live in England, USA, Australia or Europe.

I've seen this numerous times with mature foreign women and their young Turkish boyfriends. For whatever reason, they totally believe that the young Turkish stud is into them, and then, unfortunately due to their naivety, they end up losing a lot of money, their self-esteem and all faith in humanity.

One woman I knew was cheated out of tens of thousands of euros by her young lover. She was in her late fifties and he was in his twenties. She happily supported him, took him on holidays, took him back to her home country of France to show him off, bought him a car and even bought his family a house in Antalya. Then one evening she caught him in the very car that she had bought, with another woman, younger of course.

Another woman from Scotland that I had befriended was also in a long term relationship with a much younger man. He had wanted her to invest in his business and eventually she did and that was the end of that. Once the money is gone, there is no way of getting it back.

Then there was another woman I knew, again in a relationship with a much younger Turkish man. Not only did she support him and take him on holidays but she also endured a face lift so that she would look younger for him. Sadly, the face-lift cut a nerve and left her with serious complications and you guessed it, the guy didn't stick around.

A friend of mine, a kind and too trusting woman, was asked by the owner of her local butcher shop to lend him some money to help pay his debts. She had been going there for years and thought she had a relationship with the family. He had assured her that he would pay her back by the end of the month. When she didn't hear from him, she called him but the phone was dead. She went around to the shop but it was permanently closed and the owner and his family were nowhere to be seen. They had left town.

Stories like this abound. It's a sad truth. Luckily for me, I avoided these types of scams and was always vigilant to these dodgy relationships. On a few occasions, I had been asked to lend large amounts of money. This was always a red light to me and led to me reassessing the friendship. Generally, it seems that it is men that perpetrate these scams, but on occasions, women get in on it too.

On one of my trips to Izmir, I had befriended the receptionist at the hotel where I was staying. She had a son the same age as mine, she had recently divorced and we spent many hours chatting and discussing her problems. Whilst I thought that we had become friends, she was plotting and scheming over the next two years. On one occasion, she called me and said that she couldn't afford to pay her electricity bill and that it was going to be cut off. I didn't hesitate to send her the money and a few months later, she made a point of paying me back.

"You see, I have paid you back," she told me. "You can always trust me." And I did.

Then a few months later, she called me and this time she wanted ten thousand euros to start her business.

"You know you can always trust me," she repeated. "I will pay you back as soon as possible. Remember how I paid you back before? You don't need to worry."

Well, I did worry. I wasn't comfortable lending her that kind of money and I didn't have faith in her business idea either. I was in a conundrum as to what to do. She was a friend. I had known her now for at least two years. My gut instinct told me that this was not normal. Surely, a bank loan is the usual way to start a business.

Finally, after lots of sleepless nights, I called her and told her that I didn't have that kind of money available and sorry, but I couldn't help her at this time. She slammed down the phone.

I tried to call her many times but she didn't answer. Finally, I used a friend's phone to call her and not recognizing the number, she answered. I asked her why she was not answering my previous calls.

"You're nothing to me," she replied and abruptly closed the call.

I was shattered and couldn't believe this response. Lesson learned.

Discussing this situation with a Turkish friend, he told me that I had been the victim of a long term scam that wasn't uncommon; befriending the foreigner. In retrospect, I realized that she had many foreign women friends that she had met through her work at the hotel. How many of them had she conned? Luckily, I had survived unscathed.

Unfortunately, this experience left me wary, furtive and cynical. In hindsight, that was probably a good thing as I managed to leave Turkey with a few wonderful friends that I fully trust and I managed to avoid any mayor hit to my bank account.

One scary night in Izmit

As I write about this experience, I realize that it could very well happen in any city in the world but it was my first encounter of this nature and it happened in Turkey.

I had been in Istanbul for the weekend visiting a friend. I travelled light and used my laptop bag to carry a few personal needs for the weekend away. I was coming home on a late bus that arrived in Izmit not long before midnight as I had morning classes the next day.

The bus dropped me off near the highway and I just needed to cross the overhead bridge which led me to the centre of Izmit and my flat. It was a short ten walk down the main street of town to the local council building and my flat was just opposite.

It's funny how you get that sensation that you are being followed but it really doesn't seem logical. I mean anyone can be walking the same way as you. So how do we detect that we are being followed?

For whatever reason, I felt that I was being followed. If I sped up, he seemed to speed up. If I slowed down he slowed down. There were still people on the main street and a few of the eateries were still open. Still, I felt that I was in danger. Especially since I knew that I would eventually have to turn off the main street to go to my lane where my flat was.

I stopped at a kebab shop and just chatted with the vendor. At this time my shadow walked past me and stopped to window shop at the shoe shop next door. I knew now that he was following me. Maybe he thought I had a laptop inside my laptop bag. He would be greatly disappointed.

During the previous week, one of my students, a criminal lawyer working on a local murder case had discussed with the class the rate of crime in Izmit. It was apparently on the increase.

This was going through my mind. I was going to be mugged, attacked and maybe even murdered for my laptop bag. I was so close to home now. Maybe I should just run. Another problem I envisaged was the entry to my block of flats was a large metal grill gate with a tricky keyhole. It often took me a few goes to open it.

I began the last leg of my journey and my pursuer once again followed my lead. I could see my turn-off and knew that this would be his chance to strike. I had my key ready. I felt his pace quicken behind mine. My heart was pounding and I was terrified. What if I was imagining it? Maybe I was being paranoid. My only weapon of defence was my house key. Maybe I could stick it in his eye if I could fight him off long enough. All these crazy thoughts were going through my mind.

I started to walk faster and then began a sprint to my front entrance. I felt him one step behind me. Please God may the gate open first time. I pushed the key into the slot and eureka, the metal gate opened and I ran inside and slammed the gate behind me. Just as I turned around, there he was staring at me through the bars. I was on the inside and he was on the outside.

I was the one that got away. I saw the anger and frustration in his eyes. I sighed heavily. I realized how lucky I had been. I took the elevator up to my flat on the fourth floor and looked out of my window to see him walking away. How he must have been cursing himself. I was so relieved to be home safe and not another crime statistic.

A dangerous collection

It was the perfect day for a barbecue. The sun was shining, the birds were singing and the fruit trees were beginning to blossom. My friend had invited me over to his house in a small village on the Gallipoli Peninsula, across the waters from Çanakkale. It was so nice to escape the hustle and bustle of the city and enjoy the peace and serenity of his overgrown garden.

Whilst he prepared the barbecue, I wandered around his backyard, exploring and finding lots of hidden treasures. There was the rusted old body of a scooter that he had ridden as a teenager. There were various pots of herbs planted by his elderly mother. There were the gorgeous black and white kittens that he had recently adopted, lazing in the sun. There was the heavy block where he split the firewood and under the bushes I could see some metallic objects that I couldn't quite make out.

I decided to further check out what they could be and lo and behold, they looked to me like missiles or large bullets.

"What are these?" I asked.

"They're shells from World War One," he replied.

"Are they dangerous?" I asked.

"Well, they still have the detonators in them and they haven't exploded yet, so I guess they could be dangerous. Maybe an earthquake could set them off," he replied lackadaisically.

"And do you think it's a good idea to have them in the garden?" I asked.

He just smiled at me.

"You've got lots. Where did you get them?" I continued.

Since moving to Çanakkale, I had become very aware of the history of the Gallipoli Peninsula. It often occurred to me that I could be walking across the same path that Alexander the Great had taken. This region was soaked in history. The ancient city of Troy lay just thirty kilometres away and closer to home was the actual site where the Persian king Xerxes had made a bridge of boats to cross the Dardanelles.

And more recently, this very spot where I was now enjoying a lazy Sunday afternoon, and where we often explored and enjoyed the beaches, had been the site of some of the bloodiest battles of World War One. Consequently, this area was still home to many dangerous souvenirs, remnants from this tragic period of time.

Today the Gallipoli Peninsula is a peaceful haven for history buffs and nature lovers but its history is written in blood. The area is dotted with beautifully maintained war cemeteries and the local museum has a wonderful exhibition detailing the fateful events of the Gallipoli landings.

Between 17 February 1915 and 9 January 1916 there were well over half a million casualties as the battle for the control over the

Dardanelles took place between the Ottoman Empire (modern day Turkey) and the British and French armies. The Dardanelles being that most valuable stretch of water that connects the Aegean Sea to the Sea of Marmara and the Black Sea, and hence the rest of the world to Russia, was an important strategic asset that Britain was not prepared to leave to the hands of the Germans.

With the outbreak of World War One, the British Cabinet Minister, Winston Churchill hoped to end the German war effort by bringing down Germany's allies. Thus he planned an attack against Turkey.

'A good army of 50,000 men and sea power – that is the end of the Turkish menace.'

Winston Churchill

He recruited troops from Australia and New Zealand and thus the term ANZAC, an acronym for Australian and New Zealand Army Corps was coined and with the doomed mission of April 25, 1915 the legend of the ANZACs was born.

As the British, French, Australian and New Zealand soldiers attempted to land they were slaughtered in the shallows. The Turks held strategic positions in the cliffs above the beaches and had easy target practice. It is said that the sea ran red with blood.

As an Australian living in Çanakkale, it was important to me to visit all of the War Cemeteries especially the Lone Pine Cemetery which was the resting place for many of the Australian troops. Stories that I had learned about in school, came to life, such as the legend of Simpson and his donkey.

I had attended the Anzac Day Dawn Service in Gallipoli in 2012 and listened as the then Australian Prime Minister, Julia Gillard gave a warm and moving speech to the overwhelming crowd of attendees there to remember the bravery of the fallen, ninety seven years ago. I was also there in 2015 for the hundred year anniversary.

Having lived for over five years in Çanakkale, I came to learn so much more about this area from a grass roots level. I heard of fishermen uncovering skeletons in the sand, believed to be from the French landing parties in 1915. I heard about tractors ploughing their olive fields and uncovering large undetonated shells, hand grenades and various guns in the soil. Now I got to see my friend's dangerous collection, looking quite harmless as they rested peacefully beneath the overgrown shrubbery.

Many locals had similar collections of bullets, buttons, and other trinkets from this period of time. They could tell the difference between French, British or Turkish shells by the markings. It isn't difficult to stumble upon reminders of the war. The dug out trenches and bunkers are still in place and wandering along the beach paths and goat tracks one can often unearth bullets in the soil.

One afternoon, as we were swimming in the waters of the peninsula, my friend had scooped up a conglomeration of bullets. They were encrusted in coral from almost a hundred years of resting in the sea. We often snorkelled at another beach which had the rusted skeletons of a couple landing boats. There was no escaping the history of this region. Whilst today it was our playground, reminders of its tragic past were all around us and often evoked sentiments of reverence. It will always be a special place.

Earthquake!

I was just stepping out of the shower when it struck.

In my street, people were hysterical and screaming. As I ran to the window to see what was happening, I noticed the door frames moving. My books were falling off the shelves. As I gazed out my window I saw the lamp posts swaying. We were having an earthquake.

I started to panic. What should I do? I tried to remember all the instructions I had heard. If you're living on an upper floor, get on to the roof. If you're on a lower floor get yourself out of the building. Stand near the refrigerator as it would protect you if the ceiling collapsed. Climb under a table was another tactic I'd heard.

I wasn't even dressed. I wasn't going to run outside wrapped only in a towel. Maybe that was stupid. I struggled to get some clothes on, all the time thinking what should I grab; my passport perhaps.

Outside people were still screaming and that added to my panic. I tried to call a friend or two but the phone lines were dead. I felt isolated and alone. This earthquake seemed to go on forever but it was apparently forty five seconds long. Those forty five seconds seemed like an eternity.

It was May 24 in 2014. The earthquake with a magnitude of 6.9 had struck somewhere in the northern Aegean affecting some Greek islands and this northern corner of Turkey. As per news reports later, there had been 324 injuries but no deaths. There had been damage to some buildings and one of the mosques that I often walked past was cordoned off as the minaret was about to collapse.

It had been a very scary morning.

Since moving to Çanakkale, I had experienced quite a few minor tremors. The first one had scared me but then I had got quite used to them. Of course, the speculation was that Istanbul was well overdue a major seismic event. The last massive earthquake in this region was the catastrophic Izmit earthquake in 1999.

In 2009, I had spent 8 months living and teaching English in Izmit. During that time I had heard from my students, many accounts of that fateful hot August night in 1999. Most of them had been children at the time, but still bore the scars from that terrifying disaster. Many of them had lost family members.

I heard how the local ice skiing rink had been used as a temporary morgue. I also heard stories of bravery and stories of miraculous rescues after days beneath the rubble. Tens of thousands of people lost their lives during this quake. An accurate number isn't available due to efforts to keep the numbers down because of insurance claims. Yes, everything comes down to money. But we can say at least 20,000 lives were lost but more than likely it was double that.

As a result of that massive quake, people understandably live in fear of the next earthquake. Consequently, most of the injuries incurred during the Çanakkale quake were from people jumping hysterically from their balconies. Interestingly, during one of New Zealand's recent earthquakes, the only fatality was a Turkish man jumping from the balcony. That's how much fear and terror an earthquake can incite.

Turkey continues to have many tremors and quakes. In 2011 there was a massive quake out near Turkey's eastern border with Iran in the city of Van. It had a magnitude of 7.1 and about 600 people were killed. Since this tragic event, buildings codes have been revised and there are much stricter building inspections.

Hopefully, if the big one does strike Istanbul anytime soon, the new buildings will be able to withstand the shock waves and loss of life will be minimal.

It was my first experience of an earthquake and I seriously hope that I never have to go through that again.

Priceless garden gnomes

The sun was beating down on me. I was making my way back to my guest house after an exhilarating morning exploring the ancient ruins of Pergamon.

Pergamon is in Bergama which is in the Province of Izmir. From my home in Çanakkale, it is about a four hour bus journey. Pergamon is truly a magnificent ancient site to visit but many travellers skip right past it. The general tourist route is to travel from the battlefields of Gallipoli and then straight down to Izmir and Ephesus, driving right past Bergama. It is such a shame.

I was staying at a beautifully restored Ottoman guest house in the centre of town. Murat, the owner had been kind enough to drive me to the entrance of Pergamon on his little motorbike. After clambering over the ruins and descending the ancient steps of the spectacular amphitheatre, I found the hole in the fence that he had told me about and began my stroll home. Unfortunately, I hadn't timed it well and the sun was at its fiercest and the sweat was dripping into my eyes and the sunscreen was making them sting. I had also run out of water and was beginning to feel very thirsty. I knew it was only another fifteen minutes or so and I would be home.

I was now walking past some local houses built out of stone and so picture-perfect. At the front of one of these pretty stone houses sat an elderly couple relaxing in the shade. She was actually shelling peas and he seemed to be just chilling, perhaps napping. They saw me and both waved.

"*Merhaba*," he called.

"*Merhaba*", I replied.

I guess I looked quite hot and maybe a little sunburned. The woman gestured for me to enter their garden. The jug of cool lemonade on the table did look inviting. She again gestured for me to join them for a drink. I couldn't refuse. The thought of sitting down in the shade under their pergola and a glass of that chilled lemonade was too hard to resist. Plus, I always loved to mingle with the locals if the opportunity arose.

I smiled and gratefully accepted a chair around their table and a glass of the deliciously refreshing home-made lemonade. The wife scurried off inside and came back with a large plate of grapes and some watermelon. I was so appreciative of my good fortune to meet this beautiful couple who were so kind and generous.

My Turkish was still at a beginner's level and they, of course, knew no English but we still managed to communicate and have a good laugh. I was so happy to meet them both. I have found on my travels that a common language isn't the only way to communicate. We were doing just fine.

"Sprecken sie Deutsch?" he eventually asked.

I was totally blown away. How did he know German? I spoke a

little German due to the fact that my mother was German. I was intrigued as to how he knew German. His German was rather coarse but still I could understand him and now we could share more details about each other.

He told me that he had worked for over twenty years with the Germans, excavating and restoring the ancient site of Pergamon. The city of Pergamon had its origin about the time of the death of Alexander the Great in 323 BC. It grew and flourished throughout the Hellenistic period and the Roman period. From 241 BC, under the rule of Attalus I, it was the capital of the most influential kingdom in Anatolia. As a city, it grew and prospered and archaeological evidence revealed that up to ten thousand people may have lived there.

Pergamon became a cultural centre in the Mediterranean region and was filled with artwork and sculptures as well as a library second only to the great library in Alexandria. It was a magnificent city but sadly by the end of the third century AD, it was in decline. A massive earthquake, an invasion by the Goths, the arrival of Christianity, the overthrow by the Persians and finally the Romans, all led to the sad demise of Pergamon's glory days.

Various scholars and explorers had visited Pergamon during the 18th and 19th centuries, saw its past glory and had made drawings and maps, and then proposed that excavations should be made. The German engineer Carl Humann first came to Pergamon in 1864 and he saw the glory of Pergamon's antiquities and wanted to preserve as much as possible. He noted that the locals of Bergama did not appreciate the treasures under their noses.

By the late 1800's huge panels from the Pergamon Altar as well as other treasures were carefully shipped to Berlin and can still be seen today in Berlin's magnificent Pergamon Museum.

Germany continued to fund the excavations and restoration of the site and many locals, including my host, had been employed by the German government to do the work. They had received a very satisfactory wage and had learned to speak German out of necessity.

The refreshing lemonade and the cool breeze that circulated under their pergola were certainly hitting the spot. I could feel my vitality returning and I was ready to hit the road once more.

Before I left, the husband wanted to show me his garden and I was more than happy to have a wander. I followed his lead out to the back and saw before me a wonderful array of healthy and thriving vegetable gardens. Massive bright red tomatoes clung to their stakes and rows of healthy greens lay to the side. I was impressed. Along the sides of his fences he had small narrow garden filled with different coloured bushes and scrubs. But wait......what was that standing between the scrubs?

Was it a statue of a Greek God? Was it a bust of one of the ancient figures? My host was so proud to show me his collection of ancient artifacts and antiquities that he had scattered around his garden. I was speechless.

During his many years working up on the hill tirelessly excavating and restoring, he had on occasions uncovered a treasure that he thought would look lovely in his garden and concealing them in his back pack, he had brought them home. Now they stood proudly at peace decorating his flower beds like garden gnomes; priceless garden gnomes.

It had been a wonderful break in my walk home and I was happy to have met this kind and generous couple. I don't think they realized the value of their garden ornaments but they weren't harming them in any way. They had provided them with a safe home and I could only smile.

Kissing them both thank you and good bye, I continued on my way.

"Only in Turkey," I thought to myself as I skipped down the road. Where else in the world could I have had this kind of experience?

Footprints on the wall

As I rose from my bed, one hot sunny July morning, I headed to the kitchen to make myself a coffee. As I walked past the living room, I noticed something quite unusual. I had just woken up, so I guess my brain wasn't as sharp as usual and I pondered why the fly screen from the window was sitting propped up against the wall.

I proceeded to the kitchen to put the kettle on but I was trying to make sense of how the screen could have gotten from the window to the adjacent wall. If it had fallen due to any wind, it would have fallen outside not inside and it certainly wouldn't have positioned itself neatly against the wall.

I returned to the living room with my coffee in hand, in order to strategize about what could have possibly happened. It didn't take me long. I noticed that my bookshelf had been disturbed and my books were all messed up. Some were scattered on the floor. The picture frames with photos of my sons had fallen over. Had there been an earthquake?

Oh my God, it hit me like a lightning bolt. I had been burgled.

It was still very early, but I got on the phone to my friend and explained the situation. He was as shocked as I was and reassured me that he would be over to my place as soon as he could. I knew now that I was in for a massive 'I told you so' moment.

My home was a modern three bedroom, two bathroom flat in a new building. It was about 100 metres from the seafront and a five minute walk into town. It had a reasonable sized balcony on the front leading off the kitchen and in winter when the trees lost their leaves, one could even see the sea from it.

I was on the first floor and therefore felt relatively safe. Downstairs lived an elderly woman and her son, across the hall were a peaceful, quiet middle aged couple and their son and the other downstairs flat was an office. A doctor and his family also lived upstairs and the other three flats upstairs were occupied by the owners of the building. They had inherited an ancient block of flats on this site which they had demolished and built this new block with the money they had also inherited. I was renting my flat from them.

My flat faced the street and though it wasn't very private it was bearable due to curtains. The old guy, who lived across the street, sat by his window and watched all my comings and goings. In some ways I looked at that as security. So where was he last night?

In Turkey, it is customary to sleep with all the windows closed. Even in the heat of summer, my friend insisted on the windows being closed. For me, that was stifling but he insisted that it was necessary. I argued that we would run out of oxygen but he just laughed that one off. Further investigation into my Turkish friends' habits and it seemed that he was right and everyone slept with the windows closed. They claimed it was for health reasons and security.

I had come to realize that the Turkish people did have lots of customs that I must admit seemed completely quirky to me. For example; you should never walk barefoot even in your own home, cold drinks and ice cream will give you a sore throat and never go outside with wet hair and always sleep with your windows closed.

Well, being an Australian, I had quite the opposite mind-set and on the nights when my friend was at his home, I happily slept with all my windows open to get a cooling fresh breeze through the flat. Even in winter, I needed the window to be open just enough to let in some fresh air. I slept so much deeper and woke up so much fresher with fresh air throughout the night but of course, when he stayed the night I always abided by his wishes.

Last night, I had all the windows open as well as the balcony door to get a through breeze. I must admit that I slept like a rock. I hadn't heard anything. As it was the heat of summer I had also slept naked.

And here it came.

"I told you to never sleep with the windows open," he roared. "What are you thinking? Do you really think there won't be enough oxygen for you?"

He was quite angry with me.

"Is there anything missing?" he continued as he paced around my home.

"No, I checked. I don't really have any valuables. I don't keep lots of money at home and my laptop is over five years old," I replied.

Content that nothing was missing, my next biggest worry was that some stranger had seen me sleeping naked. That thought horrified me.

We tried to work out the burglar's path.

"He must have jumped onto the downstairs balcony and then climbed up the drainpipe. It's not too far," reasoned my friend. "Then after looking around for money, he must have escaped through the living room window."

I nodded in agreement, as it seemed quite likely that he had got in through the balcony. My friend then went to the window to take a closer look outside.

"There are his foot prints here on the wall," he exclaimed.

"Really?" I asked.

I couldn't believe it but sure enough, there against the bright mustard coloured cement render of the flats were his black foot prints. They clearly showed his path down again using the drainpipe.

"Should I call the police?" I asked.

"Nothing is missing and it will just be wasting their time," he replied. "What can they do?"

"We can photograph the footprints," I suggested naively.

My friend just laughed.

"It's over. You were lucky this time. I hope you have learned your lesson; you must close the balcony door and windows when you go to bed," he said.

I guess he was right and he didn't let me forget it.

A few months later, the weather was starting to cool and I had another problem. A ground floor flat in a block of flats to the back of ours had just set up a glaring bright LED security light on their rear balcony. It lit up the whole back yard but worse than that, it completely illuminated our bedroom. Even through the curtains, our bedroom was brightly lit by this new light and that made sleeping very difficult.

My friend was not happy.

"I'm going to sneak over and break it," he declared.

"No you're not," I declared.

Once again, the Australian in me came to the surface.

"I will go over and talk with them and ask them politely to turn it off," I explained.

"OK, I'll come too," he added.

"No, its best if I go alone," I replied.

I was well aware of the Turkish male hot head mentality and I didn't want any kind of trouble.

I knocked on the door and was most warmly welcomed. I explained the problem and how my bedroom was lit up all through the night. They apologized and explained why they had it installed. He had also installed a security camera.

"Petty crime is on the increase," he explained. "One night, a few months ago, we noticed a man climbing out of a window from a flat over there."

He pointed.

"That's my flat," I exclaimed. "Why didn't you call the police?"

"The police aren't interested in this little crime and by the time they could have come, the thief would have been gone," he explained.

Wow. I couldn't believe this news. We continued to chat for a while longer about what he had seen and my experience. He once again apologized for the light and made a point of directing it away from my bedroom window.

To conclude, knowing that he had a security camera and light did make me feel a bit safer and although I did close the balcony door, I still did sleep with my window slightly ajar. Well, at least when my friend wasn't staying over.

The big business of ANZAC Day

I had relocated to Çanakkale in 2010. During my time there, I had become well aware of the history of the region and its World War One legacy. As long as I had been living there, people had been talking about the upcoming 100 year anniversary of the Gallipoli Campaign in 2015. There had been a lot of speculation as to how many people would visit to commemorate this very special anniversary. Thousands of Australians and New Zealanders were expected to arrive in Çanakkale to take part in the memorial services and in particular, the Dawn Service on 25 April.

It was after all, the birth of the ANZAC legend; the Australian and New Zealand Army Corps. The Anzacs had earned their place in history as true heroes as they showed extreme bravery and courage as they sacrificed their lives in combat against the Turkish forces on the beaches of the Gallipoli peninsula in 1915 under the orders of Britain's military leader, Winston Churchill. It had been a tragic disaster with a heartbreaking loss of lives.

Sadly, what I was seeing was how everyone could cash in and

make some serious money. This would be a giant cash cow occasion for the people of Çanakkale. You could see dollar signs in the eyes of some small business owners, especially the small hotels and hostels.

A general belief in Turkey is that most foreigners are wealthy. I know personally how many times it was insinuated that I was rich. What the people of Çanakkale didn't realize was that most of the visitors to their city for the Anzac Day Memorial were middle class Australians, most of whom had a military background and they would be coming to remember their fallen family members. They were not wealthy people.

As the date was getting closer, lots of building and restorative projects were busily underway. The gardens around all the military cemeteries were very well maintained and an absolutely gorgeous show of colour. In town, lots of work had been done along the seafront and it was also looking fresh and inviting. There had also started somewhat of a building boom with lots of new housing being erected and old housing renovated. Some old buildings were turned into small hotels and lots of apartments were readied to be let on the Airbnb site. There was also a government initiative for local people to rent any spare rooms in their homes. Lodgings needed to be found for the expected thousands of visitors.

Turkish authorities had calculated that there would be ten and a half thousand visitors for the occasion. In Australia and New Zealand there had been a ballot system put in place to access who would be attending. Out of over forty two thousand applications, eight thousand places went to Australians and two thousand were awarded to New Zealanders. The remaining five hundred would be for visiting officials and important people such as Prince Charles and Russell Crowe. Well, Russell had just made a movie about the Gallipoli campaign and so I guess he deserved a seat there.

Getting back to the economics, many of the successful Australians and the New Zealand veterans, service men and their families had to return their ballot as they couldn't afford the flight tickets and accommodation. Again, I stress that these were not wealthy people.

As I know, the larger and reputable hotels that deal with travel agencies regularly, had of course, been fully booked for ages and didn't inflate their prices, well not too much anyway. The Australian travel companies that take regular trips to the battlefields secured rooms early enough, so as to not be effected by the massive price hikes.

But sadly, the evil monster called greed soon raised its ugly head. It saddened me to see this happening in a city that I had called home for five years and actually had grown very fond of. A local hostel that I was very familiar with, having stayed there myself and often recommended to travellers had raised it prices on the booking.com website from 20 euro to a whopping 1000 euro night. It wasn't the only one doing this either. It was disgusting. It was greed at its very worst. It was simple exploitation.

Who can afford those prices? It was such shameful behaviour.

Since the first Anzac Day Dawn Service at Anzac Cove back in 1990, Gallipoli has become big business but the hundred year anniversary took it to a new level.

It's on the back packer's route, even if they get drunk and sleep through the ceremony as I witnessed when I had attended the ceremony in 2012, they can still say they were there. It's big money to take the tours all year round. I don't think anyone has ever queried or thought about the huge difference in tour prices depending on whether you do the Turkish tour or the British tour?

I understand the significance of Anzac Day to Australians and New Zealanders, and it is of special importance to veterans and service men and their families and I respect that, but the truth is, today it is just a huge money making enterprise that is exploiting the people who really just want to remember the fallen.

There was of course, a lot of merchandise for sale; t-shirts, sweat shirts, hats, blankets, etc. sold at exorbitant prices by Turkish vendors. On the Australian side, there are luxury cruises being sold at over $20,000 and featuring famous singers for on-board entertainment. This is Anzac Day. Not the World Cup or a Stones concert.

I had been asked by one of the local agencies to volunteer during the week of the hundred year anniversary. I had looked forward to the opportunity to meet and greet groups of Australians and help out as much as I could. Sadly, it was a disaster. The agency had happily accepted bookings throughout the year and taken payments but when the groups starting arriving, there just weren't enough rooms for the attendees.

Imagine flying into Turkey from Australia, then taking a six hour bus from Istanbul and then arriving at Eceabat at midnight or later. All you want is a shower and to go to bed. Instead, these poor attendees were left standing in the lobby of the main hotel that had no rooms left. Eventually, they were taken to the homes of local people and given a mattress on the floor. Some people were put in a room with strangers; women were put in the same room with men that they didn't know. The heating wasn't working and some even reported cold showers. It was a total debacle that should never have happened because they knew the numbers that had booked. These were not young people. In fact, the majority were quite elderly.

For me this experience was saddening and I couldn't believe what was happening. It was all I could do, to listen to the people's woes and try and be positive. I couldn't attend the Dawn Ceremony of course, but thankfully those that did were satisfied and maybe in a small way it made up for the extreme discomfort of their lodgings.

Fortunately it was only a couple of days and then everyone returned to Istanbul and either spent a few more days in Turkey or travelled home. Still, it should never have happened because they had years to plan and prepare and they certainly took everyone's money early enough. The website Trip Advisor was on fire with people writing in their complaints and grievances. Yes, it wasn't one of Çanakkale's finest moments and I really don't think attendees to the battlefields of France experienced anything remotely similar.

How to outsmart a greedy landlord

After three years in this particular flat, it was time for me to move on.

My first flat in Çanakkale had been provided by the language academy where I had accepted a job. The second flat I had lived in proved to be too far to travel to school and so I had let it go after a few months when I had finally found this current flat.

I have to admit loving that flat and I have some wonderful memories from my time there. Sadly, everything soured at the end.

When I found this current flat, it was a huge relief. It was brand new, modern and bigger than I needed but I wanted it. Three bedrooms, two bathrooms, a balcony and less than a five minute walk to school. It was perfect.

The family that owned it seemed very nice. I did all my dealings with the son who spoke reasonable English and thus made everything so much easier. He was in his early thirties and lived with his parents and his cousin also lived there. His mother was a traditional middle aged Turkish woman wearing the baggy pants and headscarf and she seemed to always be cooking. His father was an alcoholic and was sometimes exiled from the house so I didn't see him too often.

Over the years, we had become quite good friends. Often they invited me up for some special food his mother had cooked and often he would come to my flat and share a bottle of wine with me and my friend. When I went to Australia I always brought them back some gifts. When I went travelling I always brought them back a magnet. It was happy and friendly.

The flat I rented belonged to the cousin and was in her name. So when I rented it, I had to pay a deposit as is normal and they also requested that I pay all the deposits for the gas, water and electricity to be turned on, even though they were in the cousin's name. They assured me that when I left I would receive these all back. I agreed.

Every month I paid my rent in cash to the son and I also paid all the utility bills at the relevant offices in the cousin's name. So by all accounts, it did seem as if the cousin was living there and they were saving on any tax that should be paid to the government. I didn't mind this because they seemed like a sweet family and what difference would it make to me. I was happy.

Over the years, I saw the son, who was unemployed, follow in his father's footsteps and take to the bottle. Sometimes he would become a real nuisance and I had to be diplomatic in how I handled him as I didn't want any trouble. Usually he would apologize the next day and peace was restored.

One day there was an incident and it was the last straw and I decided it was time to move on. I gave my notice and started to plan for my departure from this flat that had been my home for over three years.

In giving my notice, I requested the total of my deposits to be refunded.

"What deposits?" he said.

He had a sleazy smile on his face. He talked with his mother in Turkish and she just shook her head. He made it quite clear that I wasn't getting my deposits back.

The flat was as new as the day I had moved in. It was spotless and in perfect condition.

"Can you please refund me my deposits for the gas, water and electricity?" I asked again politely.

Again he smiled at me and shook his head. His mother sat there silently. I couldn't believe it. I had thought that we were friends. Sure, he had overstepped the line on a couple of occasions but I had accepted his apologies every time to maintain the peace.

I went away disheartened that our friendship was so cheap and that they chose my deposits over what could have been a lasting friendship.

I had let him get away with his inappropriate behaviour but I wasn't going to let him get away with this.

What could I do? I pondered and schemed and came up with the best plan.

I knew that they had been evading paying tax. I knew that any payments over four hundred lira had to be paid into a bank account for tax purposes. I had been paying seven hundred and fifty lira in cash every month.

I went to the Turkish tax website and researched the costs and penalties. I carefully drew up a table showing how much cash I had paid over the last thirty eight months and how much tax should have been paid.

I then fashioned a letter from a solicitor addressed to the tax department. I had a solicitor friend that would have helped me but I didn't want to bother him just yet. He would have been my Plan B.

Next, I listed the amount of tax that was due plus a few thousand lira penalty plus a jail sentence of five years.

I then headed upstairs again, armed with this paperwork. Again, I politely requested my deposits back. Again he just smiled and shook his head. His mother just sat there and also shook her head. I couldn't believe it. It was time to bring out my ammunition.

"OK," I said. "I have spoken with my solicitor and he has written this letter."

"Here also, is a list of what you owe the Turkish taxation department and the heavy penalties that you will have to pay," I continued.

I saw that sleazy smirk leave his face.

"So, last chance. If you don't refund my deposits now, my solicitor will send this letter to the tax department today."

I felt in a position of power. I watched his face and he was no longer smiling. He was reading the letter and checking the figures. He then related it all to his mother in Turkish.

I sat there patiently. I watched as his mother now comprehended the situation.

"Well?" I asked. "What's it going to be?"

Again, he spoke to his mother and his mother then simply nodded her head.

He rose from the kitchen table and disappeared down the hall. Not long after he reappeared with my money in hand and reluctantly handed me back all of my deposits.

I had won. He had lost to a woman, and a foreign woman at that. I felt victorious. I took my money and wished them well and that was the end of our friendship.

China product

Shopping at the Grand Bazaar in Istanbul is one of the must-do activities for anyone visiting Turkey. The Grand Bazaar is a massive, colourful collection of absolutely everything you could ever need. Shopping there is an exciting experience not to be missed. But, of course, you need to be careful and cautious because not everything is as it seems.

The reason all those lovely Gucci bags seem too well priced to be true is because they are rip-offs. Those gorgeous Calvin Klein and Armani jeans seem such a brilliant bargain but of course, you know that they are fake, rip-offs, phony. Yes, that Rolex watch too.

Those shopping for Turkish carpets really need to educate themselves before they fall victim to a carpet rip-off as many of the carpets are synthetic China products sold with Certificates of Authenticity. I think most travellers know to be aware of these scams but of course there are many that do get caught.

Back in my adopted home town of Çanakkale I was constantly

made victim to small time rip-offs but I wasn't shopping for bags or jeans or anything that may be a fake China product, until one day.

The weekend was upon us and I was going to visit my friend at his home across the Dardanelles in one of the small villages on the peninsular. He often got me to bring a few things over with me as the village shop didn't have the variety and the prices were noticeably higher. On this occasion, he asked me to go to the phone shop and buy a battery for his mum's old Nokia. He distinctly told me to ask for the China product, but of course, initially I forgot. He'd also given me the model number necessary.

I entered the shop and approached the counter. The man eagerly came to my assistance and I gave him the model number for the phone battery. He proceeded to go to the stands and find me the correct battery. I checked the model number and proceeded to pay.

"How much is that?" I asked.

"Twenty five lira," he replied.

That instantly alerted me to the fact that I had forgotten to ask for the China product which my friend had told me was ten lira.

"Oh, could I have the China product please," I asked.

The attendant stared at me in disbelief and I think he was trying to work me out.

"My friend asked me to buy the China product of this battery," I continued.

The battery was lying on the counter where he had placed it. We both looked at it.

"That will be ten lira," he replied without even making any attempt to cover up his little attempt to cheat me. We both smiled as we saw the funny side of this deal.

He obviously knew by this time that I had Turkish connections who knew the go and checkmate, I had won this one.

Yabanci

When you visit Turkey, one of the words you are likely to hear quite often is 'yabanci'. Maybe you won't hear it as often in Istanbul where there are so many foreigners and tourists visiting but if you happen to be in a smaller town, chances are you'll hear it a lot.

'Yabanci' is the Turkish word for foreigner. Turkish store owners and shop assistants can easily pick out the foreigners and this means different service and sometimes different prices.

Pronunciation of 'yabanci' is like 'ya-ban-gee'. You have to admit that it sounds like the name for an alien creature out of Star Wars or some other science fiction movie. You will be treated like an alien too and sometimes this can be really infuriating.

In my adopted town of Çanakkale there weren't too many foreigners living there. I soon became recognized as the Australian woman teaching English at the language academy. Every year the local university hosted a group of Fulbright students from the USA and there may have been a foreign professor doing some research, but in my experience there were not very many foreigners around.

Çanakkale was also the home of the Australian Consulate. Australia has always had strong ties with Turkey and this region, in particular, due to the Gallipoli Campaign and the birth of the ANZACs in 1915. ANZAC is an acronym for Australia and New Zealand Army Corps. Australian funding contributes to the maintenance of the 31 Commonwealth war cemeteries of which the most famous Australian is called Lone Pine. Therefore there were always Australian historians and researchers visiting our area but they usually stayed for only a few months.

So therefore back in 2010 the presence of foreigners in Çanakkale was quite slim. Over the six years that I lived there I can't say I had many foreign friends. I would form some friendships but then they would always move on. I did and still do have one great Irish friend who is married to a Turk but otherwise I hadn't come across any other long term foreign residents.

This meant that the few of us there sometimes had a bit of a celebrity status. This could be good and it could also be bad. It wasn't unusual during my classes for a student to just snap my photo with their phone and probably I would later be posted on their Facebook page. Sometimes I requested that they didn't take my photo but that didn't stop them.

On one occasion, I was out to lunch with my Turkish friend, when a couple of his friends joined us. Within minutes of our greetings and introductions, the woman shoved her phone in my face and took a photo. Naturally, I wasn't impressed with her rudeness but my friend explained that she had never met an Australian before. I was a *yabanci* and it sometimes felt like being a zoo animal.

Over the six years, I naturally picked up quite a bit of Turkish but was still a far cry from being fluent. I was, however, functional and could go about my daily chores without many language issues. So it always amused me when I entered a shop and within seconds the word 'Yabanci' was echoed throughout the shop. I would instantly attract special attention and would be followed by no less than three or four sales assistants.

Due to the high unemployment situation in Turkey, all the shops have an overabundance of employees who are probably working for very low wages. These poor sales assistants would silently follow me around the store, up and down the aisles and stop whenever I stopped. It was really unnerving and initially I thought they were watching that I didn't shoplift. I soon realized that they only meant to help and having a 'yabanci' in the store was a bit of excitement and broke up the monotony of the day.

If I stopped to touch an item they would quickly be at my side to help me. It was just so different from shopping back home in Australia but then that's all part of the experience of living abroad.

Sometimes being a 'yabanci' worked in my favour, especially in my town. The *Çiğ köfte* shop that I often visited after my evening classes always warmly welcomed me and gave me extra pickles and a free yoghurt drink called *ayran*.

Sometimes it worked totally against me when I would be charged double the price of a Turkish person. This often happened with the fruit vendors that pushed their trolleys along the street selling fresh delectable produce. On one occasion the cherries looked so big and plump that I just had to have them. Compared to the prices in Australia, his price seemed reasonable for a kilogram but it was only when a Turkish friend arrived to join me for coffee that I found out that I had indeed been charged the '*yabanci* price' which was more than double.

'*Yabanci* prices' applied to many things and I always had to be vigilant. As my Turkish language skills improved so did my abilities to get a better deal with my purchases but not always. Sometimes in tourist areas, prices on the menu are not listed and this is because there are different prices for locals and for *yabanci*. It was something we just had to accept. Even in my town, there were Turkish prices and *yabanci* prices for the same tour of the Gallipoli peninsula and war memorial sites.

I know that the word *yabanci* is just a word meaning foreigner but I have to admit that at times it did feel like an insult and I came to realize that no matter how long I lived in Turkey, I would always be a *yabanci*.

Treasure

"They're digging up the roads again," I commented to a friend.

There seemed to always be some road works going on in the centre of town. It was frustrating and dusty, not to mention down-right dangerous as huge diggers spun around over the heads of passers-by. This is Turkey and safety measures weren't really a major concern back in 2010. Pedestrians had to climb over pipes and trenches at their own risk and really no one ever had any second thoughts about this. It just was.

"Yes, they are always looking for treasure," my friend replied.

"What?" I queried. I couldn't quite understand what he meant.

"Well, how often do they need to replace the water pipes?" he continued. "Not so often but they are looking for treasure."

"Really?" I questioned, thinking this sounded totally bizarre.

Turkey is an ancient land with the most colourful of histories. How many different civilizations flourished or perished here? It is also said that Turkey is the 'Cradle of Christianity' and the first Christian church was created by St Peter in a cave which can be visited in the region of Antioch. We all know that where there is religion there are usually treasures.

Much further north, the region of Çanakkale had hosted many different civilizations through its 6000 year history; Greeks, Persians, Lydians, Romans, Jewish communities and Arabs. Popular local folklore alludes to a great treasure buried somewhere in the area.

The ancient city of Troy is located less than 30 kilometres away and it is true that during its excavations by German archaeologist Heinrich Schliemann in 1873, he uncovered a massive treasure of jewellery and gold plates and jugs. Known as Priam's Treasure this incredible find contained over 8000 pieces which were consequently seized and sent to Berlin. Schliemann also kept a few fine pieces for himself and his wife. There are many photos of his wife, Sophia Schliemann, showing off her valuable jewellery.

Finding treasure in Turkey is a not a rare event. Many families have uncovered treasures whilst digging in their garden or stumbling across it in the mountains or sea. The Turkish Government has very strict laws that insist that all finds be reported to the nearest police station. Those found holding on to treasures can face serious charges and a likely prison sentence.

If you're happily wandering around Ephesus in awe of its grandeur and magnificence when you are approached by a man offering you some ancient coins to buy, don't even hesitate to decline his offer and walk away. This is one of the most common scams seen around the archaeological sites. Whether those coins are genuine or not (usually not) you wouldn't be able to take them out of the country, anyway. Avoid the coin sellers at all costs.

Just recently in 2017, a British tourist snorkelling in the waters near Bodrum found 13 gold coins probably of Greek or Roman origin. As he tried to take his treasure home with him to England, he was detained at Bodrum airport, charged with smuggling and subsequently taken to prison.

The problem is that if anyone knows you have found treasure they will surely report you. In fact, even a big excavation project at your property for plumbing or building foundations will attract attention and you can be sure that the neighbours will be looking on.

These days the use of metal detectors will also cause great suspicion and the user will be carefully watched and monitored. Therefore, if you do strike it lucky, it is very difficult to go unnoticed or to receive any compensation for your find.

However, back in 1984 a TV repair man and his metal detector unearthed a treasure of 2000 ancient silver coins dating back to the 5th Century BC. It is believed that they were buried to hide them from the marauding Persians. Somehow the treasure was smuggled out of the country and it is known that an American business man from Boston, William Koch, bought 1800 of them for US$3.5 million. Today they are worth at least US$25 million. The Turkish government eventually found out and through court action, Koch had to return most of his coins to Turkey.

Another example of treasure hunting in Turkey is the recent top-secret excavations being carried out at a city called Tarsus in Turkey's southern province of Mersin. Tarsus is best known as the birthplace of Saint Paul and this city has a history of settlements dating back to the Neolithic period. Now that's a long time ago.

It's believed that an ancient Roman underground city dating back to 300BC was accidentally discovered by illegal treasure hunters in 2012 and is now guarded twenty four hours a day by an elite police unit as well as the MIT, the Turkish secret service.

On November 2, 2017 the Turkish newspaper Daily Sabah reported this:

"The excavation followed the killing of a police officer who reportedly went undercover in a gang of illegal treasure hunters. Gülbek said treasure hunters came into possession of a map of the house in 2012 and managed to excavate some 300 meters deep. They discovered a few artifacts before their excavation came to a halt with a police operation. Gülbek said an informant in the gang told police that he saw a room full of gold coins under the house."

Its exciting stuff and surely could be story for the next Indiana Jones movie.

Finding some gold coins whilst diving or digging in the garden is one thing, but sadly many of Turkey's archaeological sites have been damaged by illegal treasure hunters or even archaeologists who should know better.

An example of this is the mystical Mount Nemrut located in southern Turkey near the town of Adiyaman. Mount Nemrut is famous for the mystical collection of large stone heads sitting around a 49 metre tall tumulus. Once statues, the heads are now separate from their bodies. The site was first excavated by a German engineer called Karl Sester in 1881. It is believed he used dynamite to try and find possible treasure hidden below the tumulus and is probably responsible for the damage. Nemrut became a UNESCO World Heritage site in 1987 but sadly the damage had already been done.

'This is Turkey'

I had been teaching English in Çanakkale for a few years now and still quite illegally, through no fault of my own. I really tried to be legal. I really did.

My first teaching position was in Izmit, about an hour out of Istanbul. It was a very modern school with very friendly staff to help me on my new career path. I had initially come over on the usual tourist visa which allows for ninety days in the country.

In 2008 it was still possible to do border runs and a lot of the Istanbul schools would take a bus load of foreign English teachers across the Bulgarian border for the day to get a new visa stamp in their passport. My school promised all of us foreign teachers residency visas. We felt quite special.

It was getting very close to the expiry date on my tourist visa and still there was no residency visa. At the last minute, I was forced to fly to northern Cyprus for the weekend and renew my tourist visa that way. All expenses were paid by my school and an apology for their oversight.

On my return, we got straight to the business of organizing my residency. A Turkish member of staff accompanied me to the appropriate offices. Firstly, we opened a Turkish bank account and my school deposited $US4000 into this account. We received an account statement and continued on to the next office. Now my Turkish companion claimed that I was a family friend visiting the country and wished to stay for a year. The bank statement was proof that I could support myself for a year. That was what they estimated a year of living costs would amount to. Everything was done in Turkish and I just stood there like a dummy with a smile on my face and totally oblivious to what was being said.

Everything went through smoothly and I was told I could expect my residency visa in a couple of weeks. Next, we went back to the bank, withdrew the money and closed the account. A couple of weeks later, my little blue book called an *ikamet* arrived and I was so excited. We all thought that this would allow us to work legally in Turkey but no; inside it clearly stated 'working prohibited'.

Our academy assured us that it was OK and not to worry. 'This is Turkey' was often quoted and I guess that meant that there was always a way around things. We continued teaching and we continued to receive our pay in cash in a white envelope and usually in very small notes. I can remember receiving four thousand lira in five lira notes.

One morning, all of the foreign teachers received text messages telling us to stay home and not to come in to work. It turned out that the police were doing an inspection for illegal workers but were kind enough to give notice of their coming. Every hint of our existence, such as our folders and files were put away and it was as if we never existed. The next day we again received text messages and were given the all clear to return to work as usual. 'This is Turkey'.

In 2010 I moved to Çanakkale and began teaching at a small language academy and it was the same situation; no work permit provided. In Çanakkale it was slightly different in that the police knew I was teaching English but just turned a blind eye. Every year I would go to the police station to renew my residency and every year they would smile and remind me that I am not allowed to work in Turkey. They knew very well that I was teaching at the academy where they sent their children.

One day, what seemed to be a wonderful opportunity, came my way. One of my students at the academy, a university student, reported to me that her professor had asked if I could come to his office for a chat. They needed an English teacher in the university's Tourism Department and he had heard good reports about me. I was excited and thought that this would certainly be a step up in my English teaching career and surely I would get all the legal documentation to work in Turkey.

Our first interview went very well and he offered me the job which I gladly accepted. He told me to bring in all my documents and certificates and he would send them off to Ankara to get my work visa. Yes, finally!

I collected together all the necessary documents, photocopied and certified at the notary office. I also filled in lots of application forms and of course, the head of the Tourism Department helped me. Finally, we got it all organized and he informed me that he had sent it off. Now we just needed to wait.

Each week he would message me that there had been no news on my application and so I continued teaching at the academy. One day he called me and asked me to come in to see him. I naturally thought that everything had finally been approved.

He told me that he still had no news but that he was more than happy with my application. He explained that the process for the work visa was costly and could take five months or more and he needed me now. He asked if I could start teaching at the beginning of the next month. I queried this as I was still illegal and surely at university level this wouldn't be possible. Once again 'This is Turkey', was quoted and he proceeded to explain what we would do.

I was to come to work and sign in under a current Turkish teacher's name and my hours would be added to his time sheet. Come pay day, the teacher in question would calculate my hours and then pay me from his pay packet. Hmm, I wasn't sure that I liked that arrangement and I could foresee lots of possible complications. In fact, I really didn't like that plan and sadly decided to decline his kind offer.

There went my aspirations of teaching English in a university. As long as I lived in Çanakkale, my work visa still hadn't come through. We stayed in touch and it was in 2015 when I had just left Turkey that he once more emailed me with a new offer as dodgy as the first.

I continued to teach at the language academy until my departure in February 2015.

I scream ice cream

We all scream for ice cream.

Ice cream is good. In Turkey it's called *dondurma* and I can honestly say that I enjoyed a lot of it. In my town of Çanakkale there was one particular ice cream shop on the *kordon* or promenade that was very well known for its delicious ice cream and in the summer months it would always be necessary to queue up to buy their delectable frozen treats.

In 2009 I had my first experience of Turkish ice cream. I know that by now you're thinking ice cream is ice cream and what is she going on about?

I had been invited to visit a language academy in the town of Kahramanmaraş in Turkey's south east. My hosts had been very kind and hospitable and excited to show me around their language school and town. They took me out to lunch and dinner and really I had an amazing time there. One thing stood out and that was the ice cream. They had ordered me a cone from the ice cream shop and as he offered it to me and I reached to take, it sprung back from my attempt to grasp it. We did this a few more times to the amusement of my hosts and the ice cream man and I have to admit it was funny as well as frustrating.

Finally, I managed to catch on to my ice cream cone and the taste was heavenly. So what is different about this Turkish ice cream?

I soon learned all about Kahramanmaraş and its famous ice cream. This ice cream is very different in that it doesn't melt. I was made more aware of this on my flight back to Istanbul when I noticed most of the passengers were carrying boxes of the stuff. Now you couldn't do that with normal ice cream.

The reason it stays hard and doesn't melt is due to the inclusion of two special ingredients. The first is called *salep* which is flour made from the root of an orchid growing in this region. *Salep* is also a warming drink in winter when it is mixed with hot milk and cinnamon. The second ingredient is mastic which is a gum or resin obtained from the Mastic tree. These ingredients give *dondurma* its sticky nature.

Whilst Kahramanmaraş takes the main credit for this sweet tasty treat, it is available all over the country and is very popular. It is usually sold in colourful carts or store fronts by vendors wearing a traditional Ottoman style costume and *fez* hat. The ice cream has to be constantly churned to keep it smooth and pliable and the vendor uses long paddles to do this.

It is always amusing to see some poor unsuspecting tourist get teased and played with by the vendor as I had been my very first time. It just never got dull.

'If you kill a cat...'

When you visit Turkey, it won't be long before you notice an over-abundance of stray cats. In every Turkish city, town and village cats rule and my town of Çanakkale was no different. They were everywhere; lazing and lounging in any sunny spot they could find, stalking around the garbage bins, strutting the back streets and alleyways, dozing on the warm car bonnets and slinking between your legs at the café or tea garden. Cats are a major part of Turkish society and tradition.

It is written that the Prophet Muhammad had been a cat lover and had had a favourite cat called Muezza. Legend has it that a cat had once saved Muhammad from a snake and in gratitude for this deed Muhammad blessed all cats for eternity.

Another anecdote about Muezza is when early one morning Muhammad awoke to attend prayer. As he went for his robe, he saw that his beloved cat was asleep upon its sleeve. Not wishing to disturb the sleeping feline, he took some scissors and cut off the sleeve, leaving it fast asleep where it lay.

There is a well-known saying in Turkey that goes; 'If you kill a cat, you need to build a mosque for forgiveness from God'.

Thus, it seems this reverence for cats is taken very seriously.

Every evening, when walking around my neighbourhood in Çanakkale I would see a neighbour putting out food on the side of the road near her house for the cats. The cats would come running from everywhere, maybe twenty or thirty of them. She wasn't alone. In fact many locals make feeding the local cats a routine part of their day and everywhere you can see piles of kibble and plastic bowls of water.

During the summer of 2013 I had noticed gardeners in one of Çanakkale's council parks installing strange looking blue plastic baths along the path ways. At first we were all baffled as to what they could be but we soon realized that they were to be drinking bowls for the cats. During the hot summer months the gardeners would refill these bowls with fresh cool water.

When the cooler weather was upon us, cats could be found wherever there was the slightest hint of heat such as under the bonnets of recently driven cars or sitting upon the lights installed along the promenade.

One cat in my neighbourhood was often spotted sitting on the bench at our bus stop. This bench was perfectly located to catch the morning sun but protected from any chilly winds. Commuters waiting for their bus were more than happy to stand and wouldn't have thought to disturb the resting cat.

Other straggly looking felines took shelter in the large garbage bins which were situated on practically every street. Also, there used to be a 'cat tree' in our local park. It had wonderful hollow boughs and comfortable branches for many of Çanakkale's cat population. It was quite famous and could have even been considered a tourist attraction. The locals would put bowls of rice and fish scraps at its base every evening. Then in 2014 the Çanakkale Belediyesi, the city council, decided it was smelly and unclean (which it was) and had it cut down. It took quite a few months for the cats to accept the fact that their 'home' was gone forever. Walking through the park, you would see 10 or more still sitting on the very site, as if waiting for their tree to grow back.

Then there came another blow to the cat community, as many of the garbage bins were now replaced by underground bins with a lift up lid at ground level. This meant that the cats couldn't forage for food anymore. As a result of this, locals now placed cat food next to the bins.

There was some good news, however. A new and much improved cat house was built in a corner of the park. It was bigger and better than ever and provided warm housing as well as a colourful playground area. Sparkly cat toys dangled from the trees and there was even a shaded terrace area for summer.

There's no denying that cats have a pretty good existence in Turkey. People care for them. Restaurants will happily throw out their scraps for them, fishermen will always leave some of their catch for them and every city council considers their welfare. In every neighbourhood, the local residents view feeding the stray cats as a daily commitment and they generously leaves what they can.

Sadly, I didn't see the same love and respect for dogs. Mistreatment of street dogs was heartbreaking. Hopefully, that is changing now as many young Turks are taking dogs as pets and a pet dog is even seen as a status symbol. Even still, the dogs' life in Turkey is nowhere as happy as that of a cat.

Turkey has a long way to go in regards to animal rights but at least cats have a sweet existence there.

Dogs

The life of a dog in Turkey is a tough one.

Sadly, dogs do not enjoy the prestige and respect that is bestowed on cats. The dogs' life is a struggle from the day they are born and they constantly endure pain, neglect and cruelty.

When I first moved to Turkey I was absolutely shocked by the mistreatment of street dogs. They could be seen sunning on the side of the road looking sickly and undernourished. Often, they were covered in sores and patches of hair loss due to the mange. It was truly heartbreaking to see.

One of my first memories of the cruel treatment of dogs was in Izmit in 2009. My son and I had been invited out by a group of my students to visit a nargile café. Nargile is also known as shisha, hookah, or water pipe and is a communal smoking pipe. For us it was a first and something my students insisted that we must experience. Though not smokers, we were happy to go along and give it a try.

Unfortunately for us, the memory is quite a different one from what they had intended. Outside the nargile café, fast asleep against a wall lay a couple street dogs. The evening was cooling down and the wall probably still held some warmth from the day. They looked peaceful and innocent and certainly were no threat to us.

For absolutely no reason at all, my students began kicking these dogs and scaring them away. We were horrified at the brutality of their actions. They just laughed. They couldn't even comprehend why their actions were cruel and inhumane.

The following year, I was teaching a group of young students aged between eight and twelve years old. It was just after the summer break and I was asking them about their holidays with their families.

One young boy described how he and his family had gone to stay at a resort in Antalya. He had enjoyed it very much but the funniest thing for him was coming home to see his dog. His dog was usually tied up in the back yard. They had gone away for two weeks without organizing any care for the poor dog. They had left him chained up under the hot summer sun with no water and no food. Of course, when they returned home there was only a carcass left and for my young student, this was hilarious. I was in shock. How could a young boy feel this way? How could his parents leave the dog like that? How were the parents teaching their children? It was unbelievable that people could be so cruel. The fate of that poor dog played on my mind for a long time and nothing I could say to those children seemed to have any impact. They were brought up to have no compassion or respect for any animal.

One day I was travelling by bus to Izmir. We were stopped by the side of the road, to pick up new passengers. It was long enough for me to look on horrified as a man on the other side of the road opened the boot of his car and literally threw out at least four puppies onto the side of the road. His action was so brutal and these innocent little puppies were left to defend for themselves on the side of a busy highway. Again, this image stayed with me for a long time. Heartbreaking.

Personal space

Australia is a massive country and having lived most of my life there, I was used to the wide open spaces around me. My home was on five acres and we were surrounded by trees and nature. I think, sometimes, we took that for granted.

When we visited the beach we were lucky enough to have an array of uncrowded natural beaches to choose from. And then, whilst at the beach we would choose to leave our towels as far away as possible from any other bathers. We were used to and conditioned to having as much space as we wanted. It was normal. After all, Australia has a population density of three persons per square kilometre compared with Turkey which has over a hundred persons per square kilometre.

So, as you can imagine, this was one of the bigger challenges for me as I began my new life in Turkey. I wasn't used to the crowds and the much diminished personal space that I was now being exposed to.

I had a manager who loved to talk into my face. His face would be so close that I could see the hairs up his nostrils, the smoke stains on his teeth and feel the specks of saliva on my face as he excitedly expressed himself. I always found myself taking steps backwards but he would then take steps forward until we were right back to where we started. It was so difficult for me to have my personal space violated like this way, but what could I do? And let's face it; he wasn't intentionally trying to infuriate me. It's just a cultural difference.

Another example would be travelling by public transport which I didn't do a lot of in Australia because I and almost everyone has a car. If I did take a train to Sydney for example, I would try to get two seats to myself. We like our space and it's only normal.

In Turkey, it's a totally different scene. I regularly took the ferry across the Dardanelles and in the winter months, mid-morning it would be almost empty. I would take a seat outside to watch the scenery, feel the winter sun on my face and enjoy the ride. On more than one occasion this happened. A woman or man would come and sit right next to me so that our arms and legs would be touching. I'd look around and see that there were rows of empty seats but this person had chosen the seat right next to me. How strange? I'd pick myself up and find another seat alone to enjoy the peace but I was baffled as to why they needed to be so close to another person. Over the years, I naturally learned a lot about Turkish culture and these strange little habits.

Turkish people, in general, don't like to be alone and find comfort in close proximity to others. They happily live with the extended family in one flat and wouldn't dream of dining, travelling or even going to the cinema alone. In fact, they often were puzzled by my singleness and choice to live alone and travel alone. They couldn't get it.

Another most infuriating example of this was one beachy day in summer. My friend and I had loaded our picnic basket and swim gear into the car. We headed off in search of a remote and deserted beach where we could unwind and enjoy the day alone.

We drove south towards Ayvalik and stopped in on many beach spots until finally we found what we were looking for; an empty beach with golden sand and crystal clear waters. It was perfect. We set up our sun umbrella and towels and after a quick dip, we lay beneath the shade and dozed off.

We awoke to the sound of voices getting closer. That's OK. It's a big beach and there's plenty of space for other bathers, we thought. We could never have imagined what would happen next. Well, I couldn't but apparently my Turkish friend had.

The family with a load of kids threw down their towels and toys at our feet. They literally set up camp inches from our feet. A whole empty beach at their disposal and they chose that spot. As you can imagine I wasn't impressed. My friend engaged in some polite chit chat with our invaders and then we packed up and moved on in search of peace and solitude again. As he explained to me, Turkish people just feel safer and more comfortable in crowds. It's normal for them but so infuriating for me.

Over the years I experienced many maddening moments where not only was my personal space invaded but where I was also manhandled. Again, I compare back to Australia where we would never touch a stranger. We just don't. It's just not acceptable. I recall a news story of a woman who had tapped a man on the shoulder at the cinema to ask him to stop talking and she was ultimately charged with assault. I agree that this is an extreme case and borders on the ridiculous. However, I compare it to the many times I'd been grabbed and prodded by Turkish men. It could be in the market because I haven't bought what they want me to buy or it could just be on the street because they want to talk. It could be a taxi driver who wants more money. It could be my amorous landlord. There were just so many of those infuriating situations where I felt that my personal space was non-existent any more.

I got used to it and I hardened but I don't think that was a good thing. Life in Turkey was for the most a wonderful experience but I still bear some scars from when my personal space was violated.

Excitement on the terrace

My first teaching position was in Izmit at a language academy and I can truthfully say, that I was very happy there. They were very accommodating and supportive, knowing that I was new to teaching. When my son arrived to spend his gap year with me, they happily welcomed him and invited him to my classes which allowed him to make some new friends. It was a great start to my new teaching career.

The academy was very modern and exceeded my expectations in every way. Lessons were fifty minutes in duration with a ten minute break to be spent up on the terrace. Many of my students smoked and so this was a crucial teatime for them. They would all huddle outside on the terrace despite the weather to get their nicotine fix.

I would take a coffee and usually join them outside for some light socializing. It was encouraged that teachers mingle with students at this time. Students enjoyed the casual interactions outside the class room and many photos were taken.

From the terrace we could look out to sea and watch the cargo and military boats glide by. Directly down from the terrace across the street was a quadrangle with flag post and memorial statue to Turkey's great leader, Mustafa Kemal Ataturk. It was often the scene of official parades or assemblies.

This particular day, something was going on but we didn't know what. There were many men in dark suits, and an impressive display of men in uniforms standing at attention. It's probable that this ceremony was dedicated to the local police force as the majority of uniforms were the dark navy blue which we recognized to be police. Perhaps it was an awards ceremony as the man behind the podium was also dressed in police attire. Whatever, there must have been some very important people attending as journalists and camera men were also on the scene. It was exciting to witness this event.

Why was it exciting?

As we entered the terrace for our usual tea break, we saw that it had been taken over by heavily armed snipers.

These snipers were dressed in camouflage uniforms with dark coloured vests and dark green berets. The insignia on their uniforms and berets was that of crossed rifles and the words 'POLIS'. They also had 'Kocaeli' patches on their sleeves. They wore binoculars around their necks, hand guns and walkie-talkie on their belt and carried large rifles. It was the closest I had ever come to this kind of weaponry.

On arriving in Turkey from Australia, one of the first things that I had noticed was the heavily armed police and military in the streets. For the Turkish people it's a normal occurrence but for a girl from Australia it was quite a spectacle.

I had to get used to frequent protest marches for various causes and the always present riot police with their bullet proof vests, protective shields and weapons. When, with a fellow teacher, we had attended an election rally for Recep Tayyip Erdogan, we soon became aware that the square was surrounded by snipers on balconies and rooftops. The local residents were forced to surrender their balconies to the military for these events.

That rally had been electrifying and something that I had never experienced before. Patriotic music was blaring from gigantic loudspeakers and the massive crowd were chanting and waving the flag of the AK Parti, Turkey's leading party.

Now this military presence was on our terrace and we were all quite excited. They looked very tough and foreboding but were kind enough to pose for photos with us. Yes, life in Turkey was very different from what I was used to but I relished the adventure and excitement. You really never knew what each day would bring.

Anne's cooking

"My mother has invited you to our home for dinner," said Elif.

I was very honoured and grateful to accept this kind invitation. I had only been living in Çanakkale for a couple of months now and I had been fortunate to meet Elif, a Turkish English teacher who taught at one of the high schools. Elif's level of English was excellent which was refreshing since the Turkish English teacher that I shared classes with at the academy, did her utmost best to avoid any communication with me. She simply couldn't understand me and as I saw, her English lessons were given in Turkish. Go figure.

Elif was in her early forties and had a daughter of nine years old. When she got divorced, she was forced to move back home and live with her parents. Her parents seemed quite elderly and whilst Elif was dressed in modern garb, her mother was dressed in the traditional floral baggy pants and always wore a head scarf.

Her mother always greeted me with kisses and a warm *hoşgeldiniz* which means 'welcome'. I soon learnt to reply with *hoşbulduk* which translates to 'I'm honoured to be here'. Elif's mother radiated a warm and loving energy and I always felt very much at home when I was there.

The Turkish word for mother is *anne* and it is pronounced with two syllables; *ann nay*. Of course, Elif called her mother *anne* but I also was invited to do so. *Anne* was a wonderful cook and a generous host. She always made me feel special. I got to sit in the most comfy chair. I was always served first. She always gave me the biggest fish or the best piece of chicken. I think she enjoyed having me there as much as I enjoyed her amazing cooking.

She would slave away in the kitchen, whilst Elif and I sat on the balcony shelling the peas or cleaning the greens. The balcony was also an opportunity for Elif to have a cigarette. She believed that her mother didn't know that she smoked but I think it was just unspoken and *anne* turned a blind eye to it.

Their flat had a reasonably modern kitchen with adequate bench space and yet *anne* always chose to sit on the floor of the living room whilst preparing some of our dishes. Today she was making *köfte*, one of my favourites. She would sit cross-legged on the floor on a laid out sheet with the bowl in her lap as she mixed and kneaded the meat, onions, breadcrumbs and parley and then moulded the mixture into the most delectable meat balls I had ever tasted. It goes to show that you can take the girl out of the village, but you can't take the village out of the girl.

The table was laid with a mouth-watering array of vegetable dishes and crusty bread, all angled towards me and of course, I was offered to help myself first. Or sometimes, *anne* would just dish out my plate to ensure I tried everything and that I wasn't shy. I always felt so privileged and welcome to sit at their table. Elif was always proud of her mum and her hospitality towards me.

Elif's father was also very welcoming but he chose to sit quietly on the side either watching television or reading the newspaper. I have to admit that sometimes the television was really annoying to me as he usually had the volume so high and it was always politics blaring from the screen. I later came to realize that this was a common feature of Turkish men's behaviour. They just loved the politics.

After dinner we would move to the armchairs and lounge whilst *anne* cleared the table and prepared coffee, delicious Turkish coffee cooked over the stove in a special brass pot. It was strong and sweet but funnily enough, it never kept me awake.

Turkish coffee was always served with some small sweet treat, usually a bowl of *lokum* better known as Turkish delight. Sometimes we even had *baklava,* a rich honey laden pastry made from sheets of filo pastry and nuts. It was pure heaven.

To cap off the evening, Elif's young daughter Miriam would entertain us with her dancing and singing. She was attending after school dance lessons and so we would be her audience as she ran through her latest dance moves.

They were always warm and enjoyable evenings where I was made to feel a part of the family and I will always treasure those memories with Elif's family and *anne's* cooking.

Thoughts on work

Because Turkey has a predominantly young population, jobs are always scarce and I noticed that most students go straight from finishing their undergraduate degrees to getting their Masters. This is mainly because there are not enough jobs in their field. Only the crème de la crème are able to score the jobs and the majority of young undergraduates just hang around the streets drinking coffee and spending their parent's hard earned cash.

What I also noticed was that the mothers often took cleaning jobs to contribute to the family income and help put their children through university. There is no shame in that and is quite acceptable.

However, another common trend is the unwillingness of these young people to take any job that they consider below them. Signs for positions vacant in the pizza restaurant or local supermarket go unanswered as why should someone with an engineering degree work as a waiter in a pizza restaurant? What would people say? Sounds ridiculous to us but that is what I heard on many occasions.

This is, of course, generalizing but many young people would rather go unemployed than take a menial job. They have no qualms about seeing their parents struggle to pay the bills whilst they enjoy a Starbucks and a few cigarettes out on the terrace.

A friend of mine was unemployed and I felt bad for him as he had to scrounge money here and there to get by. He had always found it hard to get a job and made money by fishing or picking olives. He enjoyed these outdoor positions and made a few lira where he could.

Then he saw a job for a civil engineer in the paper. It was to drive through the national parks in a Range Rover provided by the company and do surveying and planning for a mining company. My friend had no qualifications and certainly wasn't an engineer but he liked the idea of driving through the forest in a Range Rover.

Despite everything we told him, he charged into the office demanding to see the manager and asking for the job. Of course, he was told to submit an application as is normal but he just couldn't understand that he had no qualifications for this job. There were other jobs in hotels as porters or waiting tables but these jobs were below him and so he preferred to be unemployed and live off his elderly mother's pension.

Another young man I knew in his mid-thirties had been unemployed for over six years. He had lost his job due to some change in conditions that he didn't agree with and consequently hadn't worked since. I saw a 'positions vacant' sign in one of the top restaurants and alerted him to this. He just laughed at me and said, "What would people think if I worked there?"

I just couldn't understand that attitude. They saw no shame in living off their elderly parents but to work in a restaurant was apparently an embarrassment. It was sad to see them wasting their lives away, sleeping in late and then sitting in a terrace drinking tea and smoking.

Young girls in a similar situation often waited around for a suitable suitor. Though they had gone to university and studied for their degree, they were then intent on getting married and starting a family. The real aim was to find a wealthy partner and arranged marriages are still quite common in modern day Turkey.

As an English teacher I got to hear many of my student's thoughts and opinions on work and it was always the same. My younger students were expected by their parents to become doctors or lawyers. The incentive was always, wholeheartedly, the money. I never heard any one student ever say he or she wanted to help people from suffering and pain.

Engineering was always the next most popular vocation and these students felt themselves above doing any menial jobs in the meantime but unfortunately there just weren't enough jobs for them.

I don't know how things are now in 2019 but I imagine that the employment situation is no better considering Turkey's financial crisis at this time. I sympathize but I still think a massive change in attitude is also needed.

'The naked man'

Life in Turkey was always exciting and one never knew what was around the corner. What began as an average day could at any moment explode into hours of madness and mayhem. It could be out on the streets in the form of political rallies and protests or sometimes it could be inside the home where circumstances totally beyond anyone's imagination could present themselves. And so it was one crazy evening in Izmit that things did seem to get completely out of hand. Well, at least moments like this did keep life interesting.

It was the end of the school week and the end of our evening classes when Diane and I decided to go for a drink. We felt like a dance too. We visited one of Izmit's most popular night clubs and set about having some fun. As usual, the club was packed and smoky and Turkish pop blared from the speakers. We loved it. We had a couple of drinks and joined the throbbing mass on the dance floor. This was always a great way to dismiss all the stresses of the week and totally forget about work.

It didn't take too long before we were joined by two handsome young Turkish men showing off their dance moves and their obvious interest in us. Together we danced and laughed and thoroughly enjoyed ourselves. These guys were probably twenty years younger than us and in excellent physical condition. As it turned out they were both trainers at one of the local gyms.

Between the dance floor and the bar we shared some conversation about ourselves and why we chose to live in Turkey. Diane was from the United States and I was from Australia and as was usual, these Turkish guys couldn't understand why we'd want to live in Turkey over our home countries. For them, the thought of Australia and The United States conjured up images of freedom and money. Australia in particular seemed to be a dream destination for many Turkish people and yet here I was in awe of my life in Turkey; funny how the grass is always greener.

The music was winding down and the evening was coming to a close. We didn't want it to end as we were just having so much fun. Diane suggested that we buy some drinks and go home to her place for a night cap and a coffee. To our slightly inebriated brains, that sounded like a brilliant idea.

We picked up a bottle or two from the corner store and hailed down a taxi. I need to add here that this was 2009 and at that time you could buy anything you wanted at any time of day or night. With the new laws, you can no longer purchase alcohol after 10 pm.

We headed over to Diane's flat which was near a military compound down-town, Izmit. It was quite high and had wonderful views of the area. Looking out her living room window one could see all the lights twinkling and boats passing through the Gulf of Izmit.

Whilst we left our new friends to marvel at the views and make themselves at home, we were in the kitchen preparing some drinks and nibbles to bring out on a tray. Gin and tonics accompanied by some cheese, olives, nuts; hopefully to absorb some of the alcohol.

Here's where things got very strange very fast. As we entered the living room, Di carrying the tray and me, the extra packets of crisps and more ice, we could never have imagined what a spectacle we were to behold.

There in front of us, standing proud, were our two new friends completely naked. The big grins on their faces soon vanished as Diane and I made it perfectly clear that we were not impressed. Well, maybe a little, but we didn't want them to know that.

"What are you doing?" boomed Diane in her teacher's voice. "Get your clothes on immediately."

Together we simply laughed as our Turkish friends scrambled to pull on their pants and regain their pride. We just couldn't understand what had prompted this crazy decision of theirs to strip naked in Diane's living room.

As order was restored and our friends were now fully clothed we sat to have that drink that we now needed so desperately.

"What were you thinking?" we asked.

They were clearly embarrassed now but began to explain what had incited this utterly foolish act. Apparently, they had recently seen an episode of a television program called How I Met Your Mother. In this episode titled 'The Naked Man' one of the main characters named Robyn had invited a man over to her home for a night cap. When she was preparing drinks in the kitchen, he had dis-robed and on her return to the room, was completely naked. This technique or tactic is supposed to make the women feel sympathy for the guy and then sleep with him. Apparently, it has a two out of three chance of working. Can you believe that?

Listening to them explain their case, we did feel sympathy for them. They had humiliated themselves for nothing. Sadly for our new friends it hadn't worked that evening but we sure had a good laugh about it and still talk about it many years later.

Have you ever experienced the 'the naked man' technique?

Breakfast with Arzu

Arzu was enthusiastic and always bubbly. I had met her through a professor friend and we had instantly hit it off. She was very much a lady of leisure filling her days with charity events, choir practice and entertaining. Her English level was not far from beginners but she was always willing to try and I enjoyed our times spent together.

She and her husband were obviously quite wealthy but I never asked the source of their noticeable fortune. I had a sense of their richness by her reference to her waterfront house in Istanbul, their many rental properties in the town centre, her water view home where I would conduct her English lessons and she would try to teach me Turkish and her glorious waterfront summer house at Guzelyali.

During the August of 2014 I had been fortunate to be invited out to the summerhouse and enjoy the cool breeze that skipped over the Dardanelles and brought some welcomed relief from the summer heat.

Arzu loved to entertain. Often after our lessons, her housekeeper would serve us some lunch but Arzu also liked to potter in the kitchen. Many times I had sampled some of her splendid soups and stews. She also baked and often presented a plate of home-made cake or biscuits with a delicious Turkish coffee to end our session.

For me, nothing beat her amazing breakfasts. For anyone who has visited Turkey and sampled a Turkish breakfast, I think you know what I mean. For those of you who haven't yet visited Turkey and partaken in this most delicious feast, I will now describe. Sometimes, I swear Turkish breakfast warrants a chilled glass of Chardonnay but that might just be my problem.

Sitting outside on the balcony, watching the many cargo boats as they glided up and down the Dardanelles is such a pleasant experience. To be enjoying a lip-smacking breakfast just adds to this delightful experience.

The table is set; white cheese, hard cheese, stringy cheese and a crumbly herb cheese. Olives, of course, green ones and black ones, exquisite in their texture and flavour. Home-made jams, strawberry and apricot. Natural home churned butter sent over by a relative from Giresun on the Black Sea, pure and unadulterated golden honey comb, plump sweet organically grown tomatoes, cut in quarters and dressed with local organic olive oil, crunchy fresh cucumbers sliced and salted. The local village bread was still warm within a crusty shell.

My mouth was watering and I couldn't wait to dig in. Next came the tea, made the special Turkish way in a double boiler and served in ornate tulip glasses on decorative saucers.

I was relaxing and enjoying the peace and tranquilly that only a sea view can offer. I could hear the gentle waves lapping the narrow beach. Distant voices from fishing boats echoed across the waters.

"Eat," commanded Arzu. "I make eggs. You like?"

"Yes, of course," I replied.

I was content to soak up my surroundings and wait for Arzu to join me. I had offered to help, but was told to take my seat on the balcony and simply relax. I could hear her clattering in the kitchen and I could smell the aromas that wafted out. *Sucuk?* Yes, I was sure she was frying my favourite Turkish sausage with our eggs. My mouth was watering and my stomach was growling but I knew that this breakfast banquet would be worth waiting for.

I was fortunate to enjoy many special breakfasts in Turkey. It was always such a treat and such a feast. Sometimes my friend and I would drive up the mountains to experience a breakfast in a village café or sometimes to a beach cafe where our table was just metres away from the sea. Breakfast was slow and leisurely and always accompanied by a gallon of tea.

If you visit Turkey, don't miss out on this amazing dining feast. I think Turkey offers the best breakfast in the world. That's just my opinion.

My post office meltdown

I had been standing in line now for at least thirty minutes. I just wanted to send a parcel home to my son in Australia for his birthday. It was tiring, frustrating and I could feel the sweat trickling down my back.

The post office was always crowded and there really was no quiet time. As it provided an array of services, it was busy from the minute it opened to the minute it closed. The post office was where the locals could pay a range of different bills, transfer money, other official business like passports and of course, send mail.

I just wanted to send a parcel. I was standing in the postage queue, which catered to those of us that wanted to buy stamps or were posting a parcel. There was also a queue for receiving parcels. I could say that as busy as they were, they were also very slow. It was so infuriating and one needed to be patient.

In Turkey, it is normal for mothers to send food parcels to their children who are studying at university in another city. These hard working mothers also regularly transferred money to these same children. I had experienced these university students burning up their parent's hard earned money on cigarettes and Starbucks. It was quite the life they had enjoying their freedom. I wasn't impressed with this new generation of young Turks that didn't think for a moment about their mothers cleaning houses to earn that extra money to send them to university but that is another story.

The queue to send my parcel was moving slowly but an end was in sight. The woman before me was nearly finished and I would be next.

Just as I was approaching the counter and about to place my parcel down, two large and hairy arms came over my shoulders and placed his parcel on the counter. He was clearly tired of waiting and I was just a woman and a foreign woman at that. I was expecting the postal assistant, also a woman, to chastise the man and tell him to wait his turn, but instead she took his parcel and began to take his details. I was in shock. I couldn't believe it.

Well, that's when I exploded. I was stressed so my Turkish didn't flow as well as it could have but I definitely got the message across. I was not going to stand for being seen as a second class citizen. I was not going to let this guy get away with it.

The rude man standing behind me didn't know what anger and rage he had unleashed and I think he was genuinely scared. The woman at the counter also looked scared and swiftly went about getting my parcel ready for mailing.

I'm sure that the evening's gossip in many households would have been about the crazy *yabanci*, foreign woman having a total meltdown at the post office but I wasn't going to be pushed aside by some huge Turkish macho male. I'd had enough.

Probably I wouldn't have had such a fierce reaction if it hadn't been for a similar episode that had happened to me the day before in the Vodafone shop. I had gone in to pay for my prepaid mobile credit and again the queue was long. After waiting patiently in line for a good twenty minutes or more, a big burly male queuing behind me, just talked over me and got served before me. I had been in shock but hadn't reacted except to say *ayip sana,* a phrase I had learned to use that means 'shame on you'. It was all I had at that time.

When I had first moved to Turkey in 2008, I hadn't noticed too many visible signs of machismo behaviour towards me. Of course, I had experienced the unwanted attention of sleazy guys, their leering, jeering and even an occasional grope. I always managed to handle it and thankfully they always seemed to back off quickly. It was worse in the tourist areas as it seems that most Turkish men are of the opinion that foreign woman are easy. As I had previously travelled in the Middle East and Asia, I guess I was hardened to this behaviour and usually knew how to flick them off.

As a foreign woman in Turkey, I had also experienced respect and chivalry from Turkish men. One occasion comes to mind when back in 2009, I had been traveling around southern Turkey and found myself in the city of Antalya. I had been looking for the bus to the airport. Not only did this kind Turkish gentleman carry my suitcase to the correct bus stop but he also waited with me, gave directions to the driver and paid for my ticket.

Jump forward a few years and manners were noticeably changing. I was experiencing disrespect and sleazy behaviour almost daily. If you were accompanied by another male you were usually exempt from this treatment as I noticed when I was with my friend but if I was going solo, it was a different matter.

As a woman, and a foreign woman at that, I felt that I just didn't matter, that I was invisible. It could happen when I was at the checkout in the supermarket, in the butcher or waiting to board the bus. I was pushed aside as if I wasn't even there. I had even been hit upon by some of my older English students.

One guy who was in my intermediate English class had asked my manager if he could have private lessons with me which my manager had agreed to without any consult with me. I wasn't very happy about this but we started our private one to one lessons and from the very onset this guy was hitting on me.

I reported it to my manager who simply laughed and insisted I give it another try. Long story short I ceased private lessons with this creep but he continued to stalk me for over a year. He would be outside my flat when I came home from work. He would send me text messages calling me 'his baby' or 'honey'. No amount of protesting or telling him to leave me alone had any effect. My manager just thought it was amusing and didn't take it serious at all. This guy was married with three kids who all lived in Istanbul whilst he was in my town on a contract with the customs department.

I threatened to report him to the police but he confidently told me that the police wouldn't be interested in what I had to say and I knew that he was right. The police didn't even respond to domestic violence complaints so there was no way they would care about my little problem of a stalker. It was only when his contract ended and he went back to Istanbul that I got some peace but he still resurfaced every now and then with some text message or phone call.

From 2008 to 2015 I had observed a definite decline in women's rights and the overall attitudes to women. What would you expect though if the political leader of the country goes on record as stating that of course woman are not equal to men. He further enlightened the country with the statement that it was a woman's duty to populate the nation and to bear at least three children.

These kinds of statements only give men a more dominant position where they think that woman roles are purely to cook and clean and bear children. If the women don't adhere to these ideas she deserves to be beaten, raped and even murdered. Domestic violence was on the increase and each year hundreds of women are murdered by their husbands.

What does this say for the future of young Turkish girls?

The general attitude towards all women in Turkey, foreign or native, was eventually the reason for me to leave Turkey and move to Spain. I'd had enough of the 'post office melt down' situations and the final straw was the constant unwanted attention from my landlord which saw me pack my bags and search for greener and safer pastures.

Facing my fears at the hamam

The hamam or Turkish bath is a hot and steamy experience not to be missed. It is a tradition dating back to the Ottoman times when public bathing was the norm. The word 'hamam' means 'the spreader of warmth' and when you enter a hamam you'll know why. Unlike the Romans, who built huge bathing complexes for thousands of its citizens to wash and soak, the Ottomans preferred smaller baths to cleanse and purify before prayer. Consequently, most hamams are built next to or very near the town mosque. You can recognize them by the large domed roof designed to let low light in and let the steam out.

In Ottoman days, all the women of a household would visit the hamam together and share in this special bonding time. It was an opportunity to get out of the house and away from the mundane daily chores. It was always segregated with the men having their own private area where they too would be scrubbed and massaged.

Besides the obvious function of bathing, the hamam was a place where the women could feel free to discuss private matters and gossip. Mothers used the visit to the hamam as a means of choosing the perfect bride for their sons. They would base this assessment on her body type, checking that she had good child bearing hips, her behaviour, her family standing and if she was deemed suitable, an offer could be made to the girl's family.

Whilst Turks may not frequent the hamam as much as in older times, they still view the hamam as a place of purification and relaxation and every town and city in Turkey has one.

My first experience was in 2007 in Istanbul at the very famous and historic Çemberlitaş Hamamı. It had been recommended to me and I was eager to experience a Turkish bath but this was so out of my comfort zone. I mustered up the courage and made a visit.

This amazing bathing complex dates back to 1584 when it was built by the chief Ottoman architect Mimar Sinan who is accredited with other architectural marvels such as the Selimiye Mosque in Edirne and the Suleiman Mosque in Istanbul. I had to see this, at all cost.

I entered the hamam and had somewhat prepared myself. I went later in the day and chose a time that would be less popular. I approached the counter and paid for the full package which included the steam bath, a scrub and a massage. I was given a tiny cotton towel known as a *peştamal* and a couple of different tokens for the different services that I would receive. I was directed to a small room filled with lockers and set about disrobing and storing my belongings in the locker.

Where to put the key? I had stripped down to my knickers and tried as best to cover myself with the little towel. I entered the steam room. I was definitely feeling out of place but I knew that I had to do this. After all, I didn't know any of these people and would never see them again, I rationalized. Its only nudity, I thought.

I saw what the other bathers were doing and so took my place upon the large marble slab in the centre. Above us the huge dome ceiling let rays of light enter through the tiny glass windows. The steam was hot and soothing and I found myself actually relaxing as I lay in wait for what was to happen next.

After steaming away and lost in thought, I was abruptly brought back to the present moment as someone grabbed me by my knickers and pulled me to the side. Consequently, my knickers came off and I was completely 'naked and afraid' at the mercy of my own personal washer woman.

This woman was only wearing a white undergarment on her lower half and I could feel her huge pendulous breasts dangling against my back as she soaped me up and scrubbed my back with vigorous force. Then it was time to turn over and once again she used this magical wash cloth to lather me up with bubbles. I felt like a child. I was worried about the whereabouts of my knickers but I still held on tightly to my key from the locker.

Next, it was time for my hair to be washed and I really worried about whether she would use a conditioner. I mean, my curly hair needs to be cared for and this means a quality conditioner but today that was not going to happen. She vigorously scrubbed my hair and massaged my scalp and there were so many bubbles. Then she poured water over my head to rinse away the suds and motioned for me to go to one of the rooms at the side to rinse myself with warm or cold water from the fountains.

It had all been a very energetic experience, not relaxing but strangely gratifying. I felt that layers of my skin had been exfoliated and I was a new woman. I also had this immense feeling of achievement even though I hadn't done anything but I had after all, faced my fears.

The massage that followed was similarly vigorous and not the relaxing effleurage I was hoping for. Still, I'm quite sure it was beneficial to my body and the oil was certainly kind to my skin. I spent another hour just chilling back in the steam room, drinking lots of pure fresh water and knowing that my body was grateful for this experience.

As I relaxed I pondered on another observation that I had made. I had always imagined Turkish women to be prudish and shy of exposing their bodies but here they were so comfortable in their skin. It surprised me that they were happily naked and even examining each other's bodies for moles or blemishes without any discomfort or embarrassment. The image of the covered Islamic woman is purely a religious choice but these women were definitely more comfortable naked than us western women. I reasoned that they had probably been visiting the hamam since childhood and therefore felt no body shame like most of us do. Another theory is that probably they aren't bombarded with images of the 'perfect' woman in the media as we are.

I was now a hamam enthusiast, recommending the experience to anyone who had Turkey noted on their bucket list. Yes, I felt a bit of an expert now. My next visit was in 2009 at the same Çemberlitaş where I had had my first experience. As Turkey was now at the top of most people's travel dreams, tourism was beginning to flourish and I noticed small changes at my favourite hamam. Of course, the price had gone up, it seemed much more organized and timed and the washer women were now fully covered up. It was still a pleasant experience but perhaps not as authentic as my first experience.

When I was in Bursa I went to a more traditional hamam and enjoyed a more organic session. It was still a relaxing experience for a fraction of the cost of Çemberlitaş but of course, not as epic as my

Istanbul experience. Down along the tourist coast you can also visit a hamam but these, so I've been told, are very touristy and cater to couples and mixed sessions. My preference is to find the traditional hamam and that would be in the smaller less touristy towns.

So if you are heading to Turkey, don't miss out on this memorable experience. I know that I can't wait for my next visit.

2009

Travels with my son

TURKISH DIARIES

Room for two, please

As my son and I made our way around south-east Turkey we had many adventures and encountered many instances of misunderstandings maybe due to the language barrier or possibly because of preconceived opinions of foreigners.

In Turkey, it wasn't unusual for a middle aged foreign woman to take a young Turkish lover. Over the years that I had lived there, I had come to know many of these women who happily supported their young boyfriend and somehow believed that these young studs loved them. I'm sorry, if that sounds harsh but I think it's fairly obvious that these young Turks were purely looking for a 'sugar mama' and a possible way out.

The reality is that many of them succeeded and got to move to England, Germany or the United States of America with their much older foreign girlfriend. I know of one young Turkish guy who married an American woman thirty years his senior and they are now living in Chicago. I don't know if they are still together. I guess it's no different to an elderly English man taking a young Filipino bride and if everyone's happy, there's no problem.

In a previous chapter, I wrote about other older woman I knew who were taken for a huge financial ride by their much younger boyfriends. It happened a lot. Turkish waiters had quite a reputation. On many occasions I had been invited out by my Turkish waiter when I was dining alone at a restaurant but I knew well enough to just laugh off their advances. It wasn't what I was looking for.

So, here I was travelling around Turkey with my eighteen year old son. Being quite tall, it's possible that he could have looked slightly older. He had a wispy moustache and beard at the time, long hair often tied back in a ponytail and an ear ring.

When we arrived in a new town, the first thing we would do is find a suitable hotel. This was before *booking.com* came on to the scene and made this task so much easier. Our requirements were simple; clean, friendly and not too expensive. Scouting around we would select a couple places and go in to the reception desk to inquire about availability and price.

As mother and son travelling together it's quite normal to share a twin room and anywhere else in the world, I don't think there would be any confusion. But this is Turkey.

We would approach the counter. We would be greeted with big smiles. All good so far.

"Do you have a room for two, please," I would ask.

She would check her books.

"Certainly, we have a very special room for you with views out over the sea," the girl replied.

We further discussed the price and as it all sounded lovely, with breakfast included, we accepted her offer.

She was soon joined by a young man and they quietly discussed among themselves which room they would give us.

Finally, she grabbed a key, gave it to the porter and asked us to follow him. We followed him down the corridor, both the porter and my son with our luggage in tow. He stopped in front of a door and entered the key. The door opened onto a rather large room with a gorgeous balcony looking out over the sea. Despite the lovely outlook, there lay before us the obvious problem.

"But this is a queen size bed?" I stated.

"Yes, and here you have a mirror," he replied.

I looked at my son's face and he looked like he was about to be sick.

The porter obviously couldn't understand why we weren't excited about the room. The receptionist had stated that it was perfect for us.

"This is my son," I stated with some alarm.

I mean, I did think that that was glaringly obvious but apparently not; a woman in her fifties and a boy in his teens.

The look on that guy's face was priceless whilst my son was still cringing at the thought.

Luckily, they did have another room for us with twin beds and no strategically placed mirror. The receptionist was most apologetic for her misunderstanding but I still can't understand how she got it so wrong. Throughout our travels, it wasn't the last time that we were offered a large bed but we learned to make it clear from the onset that we were mother and son.

Ironically, a couple years later, my partner and I were heading to Assos to celebrate my birthday. We drove around the coastline and spotted a gorgeous resort with spectacular views over the sea. This was where I wanted to spend my birthday.

We entered the luxurious foyer and took in the views from the restaurant area. The resort was built on different levels so that all rooms had a perfect view of the sea. The receptionist greeted us and informed us that this resort was newly opened and as it was Ramazan at the time, there were many rooms available. Great, we thought.

After some discussion about the hotel facilities and private beach, we asked to see our room before we committed. We were lead down the corridor and invited into a gorgeous room on one of the upper levels with an amazing vista from the large window and balcony. Only one problem was obvious; two separate beds.

We returned to reception and asked if we could be shown a room with one large bed. Apparently, as I was obviously a foreigner and my partner was obviously a Turk, we needed to show a marriage certificate. They didn't seem to approve of our friendship. This was ridiculous. We were two mature adults.

This resort, we later found out was owned and run by an Islamic group which strictly abided to Muslim principles.

We found another resort just as beautiful further along the coast and they didn't require a marriage certificate. Still, we couldn't get over the insanity of the last resort that wouldn't allow two adults in their fifties to sleep together.

When you live in another culture, you learn so much and abiding by their rules must be respected no matter how crazy they might seem. I can honestly say that there was never a dull moment living in Turkey.

Trapped

Gaziantep is a historic and exciting city in the western part of Turkey's south eastern Anatolia. It's situated close to the Syrian border and with today's climate of unrest, terrorism and ISIS, it's probably not the safest place to visit but in 2009, before the Syrian Conflict had begun, my son and I had travelled there on our adventure east.

Famous for producing the world's best pistachio baklava, with around 180 pastry shops, a massive medieval castle and a vibrant copper bazaar, we were excited to include this city into our itinerary. Its colourful history was reason enough. Both my son and I love history and Gaziantep's went back as far as the Hittites. In fact, it is one of the oldest continually inhabited cities in the world.

The word '*gazi* ' means 'war hero' and was added to the city's original name of *Antep*, after their heroic efforts during the Turkish War of Independence (1919-1923). The great leader Mustafa Kemal Atatürk had bestowed this honour as a reward for the strength and resilience of the *Antep* residents in heroically resisting the French invading forces. Hence, the name of Gaziantep was born.

One of the first sites we wanted to explore was the Gaziantep Castle, which is set upon a hill with ramparts, a moat and even a drawbridge. Inside this impressive castle is housed a museum dedicated to the Turkish War of Independence.

From the street we could see a long walk way up around the mound and under archways to the castle gates. We passed numerous bronze statues dedicated to the heroes that had lost their lives defending their city. We gazed out at the magnificent panorama of the old city and were eager to enter the castle and museum.

Passing through the massive wooden doors, we were greeted by two young men at reception; smiling and extending their arms in welcome, they motioned for us to enter. My son's long honey coloured hair and goatee and my mop of curls instantly informed these young men that we were foreigners, *'yabanci'* and in their best English they asked, "Where are you from?"

"Australia", we replied with gusto, and I entered our names and address into their guestbook.

"Oh Australia, we love Australia.......a very long way away," they continued.

The museum was dark and eerie, the only lighting being above the information placards placed along the sides and over the many bronze statues of Turkish heroes and of course, the greatest hero of them all, Mustafa Kemal Atatürk.

Following the course of the information boards and reading the history, we made our way slowly around the museum. We read about the French invasion of this region and the atrocities that had been inflicted on the local residents. We read about stories of bravery and martyrdom in the War of Independence. As we were the only visitors, we took our time and savoured the moment.

Suddenly, a rowdy pack of young Turkish students arrived and for a short moment broke the solemn mood and our reflection on Turkish history. Luckily for us, after dashing around and snapping selfies with their hero, Atatürk, they left and the harmony was restored.

Eventually, coming to the end of road, content with our Turkish history lesson and thinking about lunch, we headed for the exit. The museum was very dark and dimly lit, but looking ahead it seemed even darker. The silence was ominous.

"Maybe we are locked in", I teased, "locked inside the fortress of doom."

I was only joking, but as we got closer we could see that the giant timber doors were closed. My son eagerly approached them and attempted to push them open, but they didn't move. They were bolted, locked and totally secured.

At first we laughed. This was like the beginning of a B-grade horror movie. Who gets locked inside a dark eerie castle? We tried to rationalize our predicament. We had purchased our tickets and chit-chatted with the receptionists. We had written our names in their visitors book. They knew we were in the museum. How could they have left and abandoned us inside? How is that even possible?

We approached the front desk and there was the computer screen still turned on and showing views of the four different sections inside the museum. If they had only looked, they would have seen us.

We had one bottle of water and no food. My teenage son was always hungry and we had been discussing our lunch plans prior to this setback. We planned to explore the alleys of the old city, photograph the many blacksmiths and enjoy some local fare and of course, sample the baklava.

We imagined the baklava, sweet and soothing. How would we get out of this castle? We yelled and screamed at the door but we knew no one would hear us as the street was a long distance away. We could see through a small gap in the heavy timber panels of the door. The sun shone brightly but there was no one in sight.

I had been living in Turkey long enough to know about Friday prayer. I surmised that our friendly receptionists had gone to visit the mosque. Have they left for the afternoon? Have they departed for the weekend? The gravity of our situation began to sink in and we were no longer laughing.

We were trapped inside a medieval fortress. The cold from the antique stone walls began to pierce my body; a quiver went down my spine. My son searched through our backpack for any overlooked muesli bars or snacks. Grimacing, he presented some almonds that he'd found at the bottom of the pack, along with our faithful Lonely Planet Guide to Turkey.

It had been over an hour now. I could see the worry in my son's eyes. I was concerned that I'd need a bathroom shortly and there wasn't any inside. We again looked at the computer screen which glowed in the dark. It appeared to just be the security cameras.

At the back of the Lonely Planet was a list of emergency phone numbers and for the police, dial 155. Great, fantastic, we will be saved. I felt a little silly that we hadn't thought of that sooner. I promptly got out my phone to call the 155 Emergency police hotline.

Having been living in Turkey all of 10 months, my Turkish language skills were limited. I punched in 155 on my mobile phone. A few rings and it answered. -

"*Merhaba!*" I blurted into the phone.

The person on the other end spoke so fast in Turkish that I didn't understand a word.

I tried again, "Hello?"

More indecipherable Turkish followed.

"*Türkçe yok*". No Turkish. English? *Lütfen*. Please. Does anyone speak English?" I spluttered.

The phone went silent but the call didn't drop. I took a swig of water whilst waiting for some response. I randomly flipped through the Lonely Planet Guide. My son's eyes were intently fixated on me.

"What should I do?" I looked to my son for an answer.

"Just wait," he suggested. "They have probably gone to get an English speaker."

We waited and finally a "hello".

"Hello!" I said. "Do you speak English?"

"Yes, English", he said.

A wave of relief poured through my body.

I proceeded to tell him about our predicament.

"My son and I are from Australia and we are locked inside the castle, the Gaziantep castle," I explained.

"Australia", he declared in the happiest voice.

"Hello Australia", he continued.

"No, we are not in Australia now," I explained, "we are inside the castle in Gaziantep."

"Australia beautiful country", he continued.

"Yes, it is but we are in Turkey, in Gaziantep, in the castle," I continued.

"Australia far away".

"Yes, it is but please can you help us", I pleaded.

I could feel the sweat on my brow. I clenched my fists. My son watched me intensely. This was farcical. The policeman on the other end was babbling on about Australia and I couldn't take it any more. I hung up. Tears welled up in my eyes. I wanted to scream. Not from fear of being trapped in a castle all weekend with no food or water, but from sheer frustration. I paced the floor. My son's gaze was fixed on me as he toyed with a loose thread on his t-shirt.

"I just need a breather, and I'll try again", I told him.

I dialled the emergency hot-line again. I tried to sound calm and I spoke slowly. Once again in simple English, punctuated with an occasional Turkish word, I explained our situation. Again, it was pointless, useless, and frustrating. My palms were sweaty and I could feel a headache coming on. I hung up the phone.

We sat on the cold stone floor with our backs against the thick ancient wall and once more pondered our predicament. We certainly were in a right pickle. It was dark and cold and I didn't want to imagine an evening here. We had drunk our water. We sat silently. We would just have to wait till someone came.

Time passed slowly. My son paced the floor. He looked again through the crack in the door. I could hear his stomach growling. We longed for the heat and sunshine outside. We wanted food.

Suddenly my mobile phone buzzed. We jumped and I almost dropped the phone.

"Hello", she said. "I am calling from the police office. You called this number earlier? Please explain your situation."

I sighed. At last someone who could help us. A woman whose English sounded close to perfect.

"We are locked inside the museum of the Gaziantep castle. The reception staff have left but we are locked inside. Please, come and get us out," I pleaded.

"We are sorry for this situation. Please, relax and a police officer will come soon," she apologized.

"Thank you so much," I exclaimed.

I looked at my son and he looked at me. We ran to the big door and peered through the crack. We waited. It seemed like an eternity. Then we heard distant voices. They were getting louder. Through the crack we saw a group of police officers approaching. We were being rescued.

Finally, the huge timber doors opened and sunlight filled the dark chamber where we had been imprisoned. We extended our arms towards our liberators. We felt the sweet sense of freedom. The sun's warmth soothed our bodies. The police were laughing. We laughed too. With many hearty pats on my son's back and much joviality, we walked down the winding pathway and into the hustle and bustle of street life.

We were invited into the police station for a cup of çay. In Turkey, tea is the balm for everything. The police laughed heartily at our expense. Despite the 'No Smoking' signs inside the Police Office, I was offered a cigarette which I felt I really deserved and we enjoyed the moment with our new best friends, the Gaziantep Police.

Certainly our visit to Gaziantep is one that we will never forget.

Seriously sick in Şanlıurfa

As part of our 2009 Turkish odyssey around the south east, Şanlıurfa was definitely on our itinerary. We planned to use it as a base to explore the famous beehive houses of Harran as well a trip to the magical Mount Nemrut.

Şanlıurfa itself is an amazing city stooped in history that goes back at least 12,000 years. It is often referred to simply as 'Urfa' but after its heroic role during the Turkish War of Independence in the 1920s, it was awarded the title of 'Şanlı' which means 'glorious'. We were excited to be going there.

The first thing we did was to check-in to our hotel which was a lovely establishment that served an amazing breakfast. The only real negative, which was more than obvious to everyone staying there, was the centrally located swimming pool which was absolutely filthy with pigeon droppings. They had a serious pigeon problem which totally ruined the outdoor patio and swimming pool and I believe posed a serious health problem.

It was October and we didn't plan on swimming but it was a terrible eyesore and made sitting outside impossible. After we had explored our hotel, we were eager to get out into the city and roam the ancient lanes and alleyways. We marvelled at the old markets and the wares on display, meat hanging from hooks and buzzing with flies, cheeses, vegetables, herbs and spices, jewellery, fabrics, copper, silver and gold. It was a photographer's dream. The air was heavy with the many fragrances from the spice market. Vendors were calling out their wares. It was a total assault on our senses and we knew that we were somewhere very exotic. Long ago, Şanlıurfa had been an important stop along the famed Silk Road and the thought that these markets had been operational for thousands of years was mind blowing.

We should have known better but we climbed the stairs to a classic rooftop restaurant and ordered from the menu of local dishes. We each ordered a meat dish and of course, salads and dips. A feast. We had been travelling all day and were quite hungry by this time, so our meal was well deserved and delicious. Sadly, this meal put a huge damper on our Şanlıurfa experience and we ended up staying a lot longer than we had intended.

During that first night, my son woke up to painful stomach cramps and what followed were all the classic signs of food poisoning. He was gray. He was feverish. He lacked all energy and spent the next couple of days in bed. I couldn't get him to eat anything and just had to keep up his fluids. I searched to find an English speaking doctor as I was very worried by now that perhaps he had a serious bacterial infection. He had nothing left to vomit and yet he still did.

Fortunately, I found Emre, a young Turkish doctor from Istanbul who had just recently been appointed to a position at the local hospital. He, as he told us many times, hated it in Şanlıurfa. His appointment there felt like a prison sentence to him but he had to get through the year. At least, meeting us was a welcome distraction for him.

He advised that we only eat from fast food places like McDonald's and otherwise, to avoid all meat products. He had also suffered a bout of food poisoning on his arrival and was now very wary of what and where he ate. It was days before my son would eat anything and I could see the weight dropping off him. I was still worried but Emre regularly checked-in on him and it was just a matter of time till he would be back on his feet.

The hotel had no problem extending our stay and for the first few days my son slept and I attended to him and relaxed. I would go down every morning for coffee and breakfast but he definitely wasn't ready to join me. In fact, it took weeks before he was eating normal again and Şanlıurfa was far behind us.

We had by now become quite good friends with our doctor Emre. As my son's condition improved and if he felt up to it, we would go out in the early evening and meet Emre for coffee or tea. He showed us some places that would be safe to eat but my son still had no interest in food.

Emre took us to a newly built shopping centre on the outskirts of town. It was very modern and quite a few floors high. We would go to the second floor and sit out on the terrace for a fancy coffee like a cappuccino or a caramel macchiato. He filled us with insights about this region of Turkey. He wasn't happy to have been sent here but he had to finish his internship before he could move to a better city in the west.

"Take, for example, this shopping centre," he said.

"This shopping centre has six floors but they are only allowed to use the first two," he continued.

"Why is that?" I asked.

"Because the town planners and builders here are stupid," he laughed.

"From the third floor and up, one can see directly into a military compound nearby and this is forbidden," he continued.

This definitely was a massive oversight on behalf of the town planners and architects. How could they build a huge modern development and spend all that money and not realize the military compound next door. Everyone knows that military bases are top secret and private.

Despite all his negativity about the eastern regions of Turkey, we still had some fun and enjoyable times together and I'll always be grateful that he was there to look after my son. You never know how serious a case of food poisoning can get and thankfully I didn't get it because then we really would have been in trouble.

It always amazes me how the right people come into your life at the right times.

Abraham and his carp pool

We were in no hurry to see the sights of Şanlıurfa and our main priority was to let my son rest and recover. Slowly, he started to join me for breakfast and ate a piece of toast and a coffee but he had visibly lost a lot of weight. Usually an adventurous eater, he was reluctant to eat anything but bread. Eventually, he started to add some fruits to his diet but understandably, he remained cautious for quite a while.

We started to venture out and explore again. One of the major landmarks of Şanlıurfa was the 'Balıklı Göl' or otherwise known as the 'Pool of Abraham'. Up until this trip, I had no idea how many biblical places were actually in Turkey. One of the most significant landmarks in this region, Balıklı Göl was a popular attraction to both the Turkish tourist as well as foreigners. It is a highly revered religious site to Muslim, Jewish and Christian followers.

When we arrived at the site we weren't quite prepared for the crowds. The actual pool is surrounded by handsome examples of

Islamic architecture. Photo opportunities abound. The pool was alive with carp fish wallowing in the warm waters.

Who was Abraham? He was a prophet to all three religions. The Jews call him the 'Father of Judaism', the Muslims call him Ibrahim and see him as the Father of the Arab people and to the Christians he's up there with Jesus, though not as important.

To the Muslims, Ibrahim was the prophet who was prepared to sacrifice his son for Allah. He was also thrown into a fire by Nimrod but as he landed, Allah turned the flames to water and the burning embers into fish, hence the 'Pool of Abraham' or 'Balıklı Göl' which translates to 'fish lake'.

As these fish are protected and everyone is encouraged to feed them, their population is thriving and the pool is alive with their frenzied feeding.

The surrounding park was also alive with families enjoying the day out and sharing a picnic with their friends and family. We strolled around and took in the happy atmosphere. Once again, as was usual in our travels, we were waved over and invited to join the picnic. Turkish hospitality is the cornerstone of Turkish culture and something that I haven't experienced anywhere else in the world.

Of course, there is the curiosity. We are foreigners deep inside their country and they are curious to know why we are there. It always amazes me that even though we lack a common language, we still manage to communicate and laugh and enjoy our time together.

One favourite dish from the Turkish kitchen and which is particularly popular in Şanlıurfa is called *ciğ köfte*. Basically, it is a raw meatball somewhat similar to steak tartare. Traditionally, it is made from beef or lamb mince. Lots of spices such as a hot paprika are added which is said to 'cook' the meat and then onions, mint and parsley are added. The preparation is then kneaded and moulded into small balls. The *ciğ köfte* are eaten by rolling them up in a lettuce leaf and accompanied by a glass of chilled *ayran,* which helps with the burning sensation of the spices. *Ayran* is a delicious yoghurt drink similar to buttermilk.

I had eaten *ciğ köfte* back in Izmit but they had been the vegetarian version made with bulgur. By law, fast food restaurants weren't allowed to serve the meat versions due to the many serious cases of food poisoning. So one could only get the traditional meat *ciğ köfte* in a reputable restaurant or home-made.

We were generously being offered to partake in their picnic. After the hellish week that my son had just been through, there was absolutely no way that he was going to accept this kind offering. I could see that even the sight of these raw meat balls was making him green.

I wasn't too keen either as I certainly didn't want to come down with a serious case of food poisoning. Emre, our friendly doctor had advised us not to eat any meat products. He'd even gone so far as to warn us against eating lettuce as they were not usually washed with clean water.

Hmm, I was facing a conundrum. If I accepted their generous hospitality I could risk food poisoning and I had seen how terribly my son had suffered. On the other hand, if I refused, it would be an insult. I already had to cover for my son as there was no way he could even look at them.

I decided to take one for the team and gratefully accepted a small plate of *ciğ köfte* as well as a pile of lettuce leaves. I convinced myself that the meat had to be fresh as they wouldn't want to get sick. If their stomachs could handle it, then so could I. In all honesty, they were quite delicious and my host was so pleased and honoured that I gave her the thumbs up. The smile on her face made it all worth while. If I was going to get sick, so be it. After a glass of Turkish tea, as is customary, we received big hugs and kisses to see us on our way.

That night, I awaited the dreaded tummy rumble, but luckily it never came. I had survived and I was up to eat another hearty breakfast at our hotel.

The beehive houses of Harran

Not far from Şanlıurfa and very close to the Syrian border, lying between the Tigris and Euphrates rivers is the town Harran. It is famous for the unusual conical dome roofed houses known as beehive houses. A lack of timber in the region, led to these houses being fully constructed out of mud bricks that had been dried out in the sun. The dome roof design assisted in keeping these homes warm in winter and cool in summer.

This style of house is believed to have been built and inhabited since as far back as 2500BC, though because of the building materials these houses last no longer than 150 years at most. Today, some of the houses are family dwellings but others are converted into tea shops for the tourists.

We were excited to visit this historic town and see for ourselves. It seems everywhere in Turkey is a photographer's dream, and here was no different. From the minute we stepped off the bus, photo opportunities presented themselves: a couple camels tied up to a fence and their colour blending perfectly into the tan- coloured earth of this region.

From the moment we got off the bus we were also mobbed by locals wanting to be our guides. They were very insistent and wouldn't take 'no' for an answer. This was in 2009 and there was a new building near the entrance which had lovely clean toilets as I recall. Our would-be guides waited for us outside and it took a bit of effort to lose them.

I might mention here that when travelling around the south east of Turkey back then, finding a clean modern toilet was a real win. Usually, all that was on offer were smelly filthy hole in the ground toilets that you straddled and I always managed to wet the legs of my jeans. Perhaps, that was too much information.

Anyway, by leaving through another exit we managed to lose our stalkers and head towards the main part of town. It was obvious that work was being done at this time to improve the site for the increase of tourists. By now, ten years later, I'm quite sure that Airbnb would have made its mark here as the tourist dollar started to flow.

We walked the dusty roads and headed to our first beehive house. It was open for inspection and definitely set up for tourists. It was, after all, a very interesting form of housing somewhat like a more solid and permanent form of tent. We were told that another important feature of these houses was their ability to be constructed fast and therefore suited the nomadic lifestyle of the people of this region.

Inside, the mud walls were adorned with pottery and Turkish carpets and cushions. Lots of colourful trinkets also hung around the wall and a few of the beehive houses had these wares for sale. Outside was the wagon wheel, large pottery vases, some tools and maybe a donkey tied up. It presented a very unique style of living and made for great photos.

One thing that really shocked us was the piles and piles of

garbage around every corner. There could be goats tied up grazing on what little greens they could find and surrounded by colourful plastics and water bottles. Such a shame.

Further exploring and we came upon the remains of a city wall and a castle. We climbed to the top and rambled through the ruins. Suddenly, out of no where, I received a hard blow to my back. Then a shower of stones followed. We were under attack by a group of local youth. They were laughing and picking up more stones to throw. They seemed to be around ten or twelve years old, so young and so angry.

I don't know if they realized how painful a small stone to the body was. I yelled at them and they just laughed more and more. We had to escape and hopefully not take a blow to the head. Thankfully, they didn't follow us. They had an excellent hideout in this ancient fortress and they probably just waited for the next innocent tourist to stumble along.

Arriving back into the main part of town, we decided to enter one of the beehive houses that was operating as a tea house. By now we were hot and weary and definitely deserved a rest and a refreshment. It was decidedly cooler inside the beehive house. It was heaven. We both decided on a refreshing *ayran*. This yoghurt drink is very popular all over Turkey but its especially delicious in the south-east.

I took this opportunity to check myself for bruises from our recent stone attack. Some of the contact spots still had a little sting in them. My son also had received a hit or two. Dangerous games those boys were playing.

Inside, the tea shop was beautifully decorated with colourful Turkish carpets and kilims. Large pottery pots stood in corners and timber tables and chairs filled the centre. Soon a young lady joined us and politely took our order. She was dressed in the traditional clothes of this region; a long following skirt with a floral apron, plain jumper and flowery headscarf. Her features were hardened and I noticed her thick dark eyebrows. The extreme weather conditions out here would surely have a negative effect on one's skin, I thought. She was fast and efficient and spoke very good English.

I began talking with her as I was interested in her life here. She was happy to answer my questions and I answered hers. Coming from Australia always gets a big reaction. People are amazed at how far away it is and they've seen it on TV and imagine it to be the ultimate paradise.

She was born and raised here in Harran. She now worked for her father serving tea and coffee to tourists like us. Basically, she hated it and dreamed of getting away. She mentioned some American soap operas that she watched on the internet and I think this had bred the uneasiness and restlessness that she felt. She dreamed of living in a modern house like what she saw on the TV programs. I tried to tell her that those shows painted a pretty picture but it wasn't always like that.

She had taught herself English from the internet and from the tourists. She hadn't been allowed to go to school as there was always work to do. I felt for her and her future. She was destined for marriage and babies and working in the family business.

This was a perfect example of how the internet has allowed people from all over the world to connect but it has also caused the resentment that some people living in more primitive conditions are feeling. Its understandable that this young lady would desire the life she sees on the internet and because its out of reach, a bitterness grows. Tourists are just a means of making money, but I don't imagine they are liked which is evident in our earlier stone throwing attack.

Sometimes, we forget how fortunate we are to travel the world and to step in and out of these people's existence, whilst for them there is no way out. For example, what a difference in circumstances between that young girl's life and my son's.

We spent the rest of the day wandering the dusty lanes and taking lots of photos, before we boarded the bus for our journey back to Şanlıurfa. Another awesome day in south-east Turkey but I carried a sadness for that young girl who wanted so much for her life than was possible.

Sunset at Mount Nemrut

Mount Nemrut or *Nemrud Dağı,* as its called in Turkish, was one place we had dreamed of visiting for quite a while. It seemed like a magical and mysterious place. Like the Pyramids of Giza, Mount Nemrut posed many similar questions and ponderings. How did these massive stone statues get to be on the top of a mountain? Had they been constructed there or had they been carried up?

Mount Nemrut is 2,134 metres above sea level and one of the highest peaks of the Taurus mountains in Mesopotamia. It is located about 180 kilometres from Şanlıurfa. The usual starting off place for visiting this region is Adiyaman but as we were still in Şanlıurfa, we decided to hire a 4WD vehicle and driver and make a big day of it.

It was about a three hour drive there. Our goal was to reach the summit for sunset when it is the optimum time to experience the majesty of these mysterious stone statues against the backdrop of the surrounding mountains draped in the glorious glow of dusk. It was also prime time for taking photos.

We had negotiated a price with our driver which we knew was overpriced but we were excited and it seemed the best option for us. He was going to stop and show us some other lesser known sights along the way and we would also stop at a local restaurant for lunch. It was an early start and we were on our way.

The drive itself was awesome, passing through picturesque countryside and true to his word, he did show us some sights that were well worth seeing. We stopped at the Septimius Severus Bridge or *Cendere Köprüsü* as its known in Turkish. This impressive single arch Roman bridge was built between the years of 193 – 211 AD in honour of the Roman Emperor Lucias Septimius Severus. It crosses the Cendere river, hence its Turkish name.

It was a wonderful photo opportunity and that's when out of the blue, our driver asked my son if he needed the toilet and whether he needed to do a number one or a number two? This was so random and amusing but horribly embarrassing for my son. Plus, there were no toilets in sight so we still wonder what prompted this question. Just a funny little memory that stays with you all these years later.

Further along our way, we stopped at the ancient site of Arsameia, a former Greek settlement founded in 2nd century BC. A well preserved stone relief of the Greek God Hercules shaking hands with King Mithridates, father of Antioches, as well as another huge slab of stone covered with ancient Greek hieroglyphics, guarded the entrance to a very impressive 158 metre deep tunnel or cave. It was very steep and dark down there so we didn't explore further but again it was an amazing photo stop. How incredible was the history of this country? I was constantly in awe.

Our lunch stop was, of course, part of the deal we had struck with our driver and naturally, where he brought all his clients. The owners of the establishment welcomed him heartily with slaps on the back and merriment as they eyed us up and down. We did feel a bit like lambs to the slaughter.

After introductions, we took our seats at a rustic timber table beside a babbling brook and to be honest, it was an extremely pleasant setting. Icy cold soft drinks were welcome as we were feeling parched from the long drive and our clambering over the rocks at Arsameia. It was October but the sun was still rather fierce.

Generous portions of fish and rice were served and we settled down to enjoy our lunch. Memorable, was the conversation we had with one of the elders from this cozy lunch stop. You couldn't really call it a restaurant but more like a family kitchen serving delicious home cooked fare.

The elderly gentleman came and joined us and began to recount his memories of Mount Nemrut. It had been his playground as a child and as he grew older he had witnessed numerous archaeologists visit the site. He had even worked for some of them.

Atop of Mount Nemrut is a giant tumulus believed to be the tomb of King Antiochus 1 of the Commagene Empire which had controlled this area from 109 BC to 72 AD. It was also believed that within this tumulus was hidden inconceivable treasures. Thus, archaeologists of the day were more interested in finding the treasure than preserving the majestic statues that guarded the mound. He explained how dynamite had been used and that some damage to the giant heads was a result of these efforts to uncover the riches. How sad was that? As of our visit in October 2009, I don't think any treasure has yet been unearthed and thankfully modern day archaeologists are more concerned with preserving the history.

Other damage to the noses of the giant head statues is believed to be due to vandalism as a rejection of the religious images these statues may have represented. Earthquakes and environmental forces have also played their part in causing erosion of the tumulus. Add to this the impact of tourism, which ten years after our visit, now sees more than 50,000 visitors a year trampling around the site.

The conversation had been enthralling and our lunch had hit all the right spots. We were ready now to hit the road and reach the peak by sunset. Our excitement was palpable as we finally reached our destination. We had chatted on a bit long at lunch and now it was a race to scramble up the path to reach the summit before sunset but we made it.

Less than ten people were already there enjoying the silence and atmosphere. Its hard to put into words, but there was a stillness and serenity to being there at this time of the day, almost a religious experience. There was the realization of how small and insignificant we really are on this planet. What mysteries abound? What was the story here? How did these statues, some of them weighing up to 9 tonne get to be sitting on the top of this mountain?

Were we in a film shoot for an Indiana Jones movie or perhaps Land Before Time? We sat and absorbed the atmosphere and splendour as the colours of the fading sun highlighted the magnificence of Mount Nemrut.

What a day! It really had been a memorable day and wearily we trusted our driver to take us home.

Welcome to Mardin

Whilst teaching in Izmit, I had met a young man from Mardin. He was a delight to talk with and as with most Turks, he was fiercely proud of his city. He explained to us its location in south-eastern Turkey and a stone's throw from the Syrian border. His warm invitation to visit his home town was something we could seriously consider as we had planned to travel that way. And, how nice to have someone to show us around.

As our bus pulled into the bus station which was situated down in the new city, Mehmet was there to meet us.

"Welcome to my city," he proudly declared. "Mardin welcomes you."

It had been a reasonable three hour bus ride but we were hot and weary. We were grateful and relieved to have Mehmet meet us and guide us to our accommodation. It took all the thinking out of navigating our way and God knows, how hopeless I am with maps.

We had booked a room in the Mardin Öğretmen Evi or Teachers' House. Most cities in Turkey have these establishments and they are usually housed in grand old buildings with massive rooms and high ceilings. They are very economical and cater to teachers travelling for conferences or school activities. As I was an English teacher, I was also welcome there but at a slightly higher rate. It still offered excellent value as the rooms were always immaculate and comfortable. Breakfast was also included and I always needed my morning coffee.

After settling in and getting organized, Mehmet took us to his home and we were warmly welcomed by his family and friends. There was quite a small gathering and they had prepared a meal for us. Sitting in a large circle on floor cushions around a massive shallow pan of lamb casserole, we chatted and laughed and got to know each other.

I wasn't entirely comfortable eating this way and also the sight of the meat wasn't to my liking but I grinned and bared it, grateful for the generous effort that had been made in our honour. How fortunate we were.

Tea was now served and we were entertained by Mehmet playing traditional local music on his saz, a seven stringed musical instrument somewhat like a guitar but with a large bellied body. His young nephew was dancing and throwing himself around the cushions much to everyone's delight. It was a privilege to be a part of this family time in Mardin.

Later that afternoon Mehmet was keen to take me to his English school to introduce me to the director. This was another pleasant encounter that came with a job offer. The school was new and modern, located in the old town but I knew from the bus ride in that this wasn't an area I'd like to live; sizzling hot summers and freezing winters. Thank you for the offer but no thanks.

The following morning we were eager to explore the old town.

Perched up on a hill, the old town was a conglomeration of old and restored sand coloured stone buildings that gently spilled down towards the new town. Looking out from various vantage spots, a dusty sandy desert known as the Mesopotamian Plain spread out endlessly before us. It was spectacular.

Local limestone was the main building material of the area. The architecture of this historic city was impressive; straight lines, attractive designs with intricate facades. A combination of influences from the Assyrian, Turkish, Kurdish and Arab cultures. The colours of stone blended perfectly into their surroundings making it a very captivating city.

Most impressive of all was the Deyr-ul Zafaran Monastery of a Syrian Orthodox origin and dating back at least 1500 years. There are many other religious monuments to visit as well as the Great Mosque with its massive minaret but for us the excitement was exploring the ancient stoned alleyways of the exotic Arabic souk. We trod the path of the ancient Silk Road merchants and we wandered among the herbs and spices, nuts and seeds, fruits and vegetables, freshly slaughtered meat hanging from hooks, goats heads and gizzards, brightly coloured carpets, shoes, reels of cloth and clothes, bales of tobacco and copper goods. You name it, you could find it there.

The food was another highlight. We feasted well on the local cuisine whilst enjoying the views from rooftops and terraces. One place that had been highly recommended by our Lonely Planet travel Guide was a restaurant that was apparently an all- female endeavour. We decided to have our dinner there and watch the sunset over the Mesopotamian plains. The views from the terrace were spectacular and we were happy to order a wine and relax in the ambiance of the setting. Despite being advertised as a restaurant ran by women, the waiter was a man. He soon brought to our table a basket with a folded napkin that appeared to contain warm bread fresh from the oven. I excited opened up the napkin to take a piece and was just about to take a bite, when my son cried out, "Stop."

Alarmed, I dropped the piece of bread and soon saw what he had seen. Its underside was covered in mould, green, gray, furry mould. How could they serve this? Surely they knew? Thanks, Lonely Planet.

We waited for the waiter to come our way and showed him the bread. He just shrugged his shoulders and took it way. No apology. No explanation. We weren't amused and decided to leave. I'm sure our experience to that highly rated restaurant was not the norm but still we were left feeling cheated by the Lonely Planet recommendations.

Our few days in Mardin had been a wonderful experience and we had met some kind and hospitable people like Mehmet and his family. It was time to move on to explore new horizons. Our next adventure, the incredible and soon to be destroyed Hasankeyf.

Keep Hasankeyf Alive

'Keep Hasankeyf Alive' is the initiative of an organization in south eastern Turkey that is fighting to save this remarkable 11,000 year old settlement and ancient citadel from destruction. Imagine a township that has been continually inhabited since the Neolithic times. As long as Damascus in Syria. Imagine the history, the culture and the insights into the lives of those cave dwellers, all to be lost beneath 60 metres of water when the Ilisu Dam is finally completed. What a crime.

Hasankeyf is an impressive settlement and complex of caves on the Tigris River in the Batman district of south-east Turkey. My son and I included it on our adventure to these parts in late 2009. At that stage, we were ignorant to the politics and imminent future of Hasankeyf. We were simply exploring the region and it was a chance meeting on a bus with one of the main activists that convinced us we needed to see this slice of Turkish history.

The girl we met informed us of the plans to build the dam on the Tigris River which would completely flood and destroy this ancient site. Local people would lose their homes and livelihoods. They were to be resettled in different areas and taken away from the only life and existence they had known. It was to be a massive tragedy. All is never as it seems and she told us how the construction of a dam there would not be that necessary and probably wouldn't have a lifespan of more than 100 years, but the main motivation was to cut off the water supply to northern Iraq.

This young woman also gave us a book which she was involved in producing. I still treasure this book as it isn't readily available in shops and it was a special gift for us.

So, book in hand, off we went to explore Hasankeyf. Our first port of call was the ancient bridge that crossed the Tigris. Built in 1116, it replaced the older original bridge. One can only imagine the ancient merchants and tradesmen hauling their loads across the river on the famed Silk Road.

We roamed the dusty lanes and explored some of the caves. Some of the caves were still inhabited and some housed small tea shops or cafes. It was late October but the sun still had some heat in it as we climbed and followed the steep trails. I can remember stopping at one of these cafes, high up in the cliffs, and enjoying the refreshing yoghurt drink known as '*ayran*'. It was served in a rather large ornate copper bowl and we laughed as both of us were left with white frothy moustaches. It was delicious.

Further climbing and exploring brought us to an ancient cemetery and more fascinating archaeological sites. The whole area is just a treasure trove of antiquities and relics of bygone days; a living museum.

After a day of exploring, we wandered down to the river and chose to sit at one of the many fish restaurants. A string of restaurants lined the edge of the Tigris, all similarly built with little ladders up to these timber structures built over the flowing waters. It felt exciting and exotic; enjoying a feast of freshly caught trout. A gaggle of geese noisily sought our attention at the bottom of the ladder. We decided it was safer to stay up on the platform and enjoy another glass of Turkish wine rather than have to fight off these hungry looking geese.

Sadly, those fish restaurants are long gone now as the works have begun on the dam project. We are saddened by what we see and hear in the news. Luckily for my son and me, we did get to visit and experience the wonder of this area, a place we will never forget.

Urged on by our new friend, to try and bring attention to their cause back in 2009, I did send an email to the Australian television program Foreign Correspondence. I thought that they might be interested in such a tragic story but unfortunately they never replied. Ironically, in 1981, Turkey had declared this area a natural conservation site, but I guess big money and politics changes all that.

As I write, the destruction of the cliffs and caves has begun. The Turkish government has said that it has done everything in its power to save the priceless ancient monuments. In August 2018 the Artuklu Hamam bath house was loaded on to a truck and relocated to a safe place. Similarly, remnants of the 14th century Ayyubid mosque were also relocated. However, these feeble attempts to save a couple important cultural monuments don't address all the other amazing antiquities from so many different ancient civilizations that lay buried beneath the earth waiting to be uncovered.

What a pity.

Our visit to the Diyarbakir Military Base

When I first began my teaching career in Izmit, it was scary. However, it was made easier by the wonderful students that I got to teach and know. From one of my very first classes, one student stood out and was to become a close friend to my son and me.

Mert was an intelligent and fun student to have in class. He was always cooperative and eager to contribute to our lessons. He never shied away from any opportunity to air his opinions on whatever topic that we were discussing. Often, when the rest of the class sat there in silence, Mert brought life and humour to the class.

Mert was a heavy metal enthusiast. In fact, at the time, he also deejay-ed a heavy metal program on a local radio station. Mert's appearance was black. He wore black jeans, black t-shirts, black boots, black hair, full black beard, tattoos and numerous piercings. He looked tough but he was the sweetest guy.

My son was soon to arrive in Turkey to spend his gap year with me. Naturally, I told my classes about him and Mert stepped up to be his companion and friend. I think at the time Mert was twenty one or twenty two years old and my son was eighteen years old, so not too much of an age difference. Whilst Mert could show my son around, he could also practice his English. It was a win, win and I was happy to introduce my son to him.

The first meeting was hilarious. As is normal with a Turkish greeting, Mert went in to kiss my son on the cheeks. My son, not familiar with anything Turkish yet, pulled away. After explaining that this was the usual greeting he was fine and over the year he spent in Turkey, it just became a normal practice to him.

One of their first excursions was to a heavy metal club in Taksim. I trusted both Mert and my son, so I wasn't at all worried and they came home at a reasonable hour. They had lots of fun adventures together and had become close friends.

Then, Mert had to go to do his military service. In Turkey, military service is a compulsory duty of all young men unless their families are wealthy enough to buy them out of that obligation. Mert's family was not and so off he went to serve out his time in the city of Diyarbakir, in south eastern Turkey.

At that time, with the heat of the Kurdish conflict very much alive, Diyarbakir was quite a dangerous place to be. Random bombings and terrorist attacks were frequent. Saying goodbye to Mert was sad but we promised him that we would visit him. He would be far away from his family and friends and it had to be a daunting experience. His mother would fly over once or twice to see him but that was an expense she couldn't really afford.

When the young men are assigned their military postings, they usually travel by bus and often at the bus stations there is a large crowd gathered to see them off and car horns and commotion follow. Its loud and chaotic but perhaps a welcome send off for these young men. The reality is that some of them may never return home. There was a war with the Kurds that claimed many lives on both sides at that time and even today there are many casualties along the borders.

So Mert went off to serve his military duty and it was a few months later that we got the opportunity to visit him. We had visited Mardin and then continued on to Batman to visit Hasankeyf before they flooded it, and Diyarbakir was in this vicinity.

Diyarbakir is considered to be the unofficial capital of Northern Kurdistan, an area that the Turkish government doesn't recognize. As with all of Turkey, Diyarbakir has a colourful history dating back to the Stone age. Of course, we roamed around to see the sights and enjoy the local cuisine but our main objective was to find the military base and surprise Mert.

We were excited. We knew he would be so surprised. We started out early to visit the base. Met at the gate, we were asked our business and asked to wait whilst they confirmed the information that we had given them.

Next, we had to relinquish our bags, mobiles phones and cameras which was totally understandable. Then my son was given given a full body frisk by a very handsome young soldier. After he was done, I approached with my hands up but this provoked much laughter and merriment among the guards. Apparently, much to my disappointment, it wasn't regulation to frisk women.

We were guided into a garden area with picnic tables and benches and we saw many young soldiers meeting up with their loved ones. Mothers especially, would travel large distances to visit their sons and bring them some home-made treats. We'd brought some chocolate bars.

We waited patiently observing our surroundings and looking out for Mert to appear. There he was. When he saw us, he came running, tears streaming down his cheeks. He was so happy to see us and we felt so happy that we had made the effort.

Was this really Mert? How he had changed. All his black hair was gone. He sported a close shaved head and no sign of any facial hair. The piercings were all gone. He looked smaller. He looked like a little boy playing dress-ups. His uniform was a couple sizes too big as were his boots, which were causing him problems. He seemed to have lost his confidence and outgoing personality. He was sad.

He brought us tea as is customary in Turkey. We sat and talked. He mentioned that yesterday had been his day off and we could have left the base together but we hadn't known that. We were slightly upset about that. He told us how his day started very early and he had been cutting the grass with scissors. What? We were astounded. Menial chores were given to keep the young recruits in line.

We told him about our travels and our adventures. It was a good couple hours we spent together until it was time to leave. We felt so sad leaving him there and wished we could have sneaked him out with us. We said our goodbyes. We hugged. He thanked us so much for our visit and we were on our way.

We wondered what hardships he had endured there because he wasn't the cheerful heavy metal rocker that we had come to know and love. He seemed broken.

The rest of day was solemn. Our hearts felt heavy. We realized how lucky we were that my son wasn't forced into military service in Australia.

TURKISH DIARIES

2010 – 2015

My solo travels

TURKISH DIARIES

Istanbul, Istanbul

For most people visiting Turkey, Istanbul is their first port of call. It certainly was for me. As the years went by, my relationship with Istanbul was one of love and hate. Probably, a lot more love than hate but Istanbul can be overwhelming and oppressive and sometimes you just want to get out of there. Other times, its filled with magic and charm.

Have a listen to the song 'Istanbul, Istanbul Olali' by Sezen Aksu. Even if you don't understand the words, this love song to Istanbul is haunting and evocative. One of the first Turkish musicians that I was introduced to, Sezen Aksu soon became my favourite. Known as the 'Turkish Queen of Pop' I never thought this title did her justice. Sure, she has some pop songs but she also has some deep and soulful melodies that warm you to the core. 'Istanbul, Istanbul Olali' is one of them.

My first visit to Istanbul was in 1985 with my ex husband. At that time, Istanbul was definitely exotic and totally captivating. It felt a lot more Asian than European. In 1978, the movie 'Midnight Express' had been released and we know now that the allegations in the book on which it was based weren't true but in 1985, the reputation and infamy were still ripe. This gave Istanbul the thrill factor. So, of course, we visited the infamous 'Pudding Shop' where all the beatniks and hippies of the '60s had hung out and where all the drug deals had apparently been done. Today, the 'Pudding Shop' is a totally new establishment and really there is no reminder of that terrifying prison drama.

I also remembered the gold. So much gold in the famous Grand Bazaar. It was mind blowing to us and my photos from that time reflect just how impressed we were with the Grand Bazaar. We didn't buy gold or leather or carpets but they had sure tried to convince us that we needed to.

Other memories of Istanbul back then were of families picnicking in the park, babies rocking in makeshift hammocks whilst theirs mothers prepared the salads and their fathers grilled the meat. Family is family where ever you are, enjoying the simple pleasures in life.

Down at the waterfront I remember getting our motorbike boots polished for a song before we rode our bike onto the car ferry headed for Izmir. That car ferry doesn't run any more but back then it saved us a massive ride as we headed down the coast.

If you've read my first book *'A Turkish Affair'* you'll know that the next time I visited Istanbul was in 2007. I was reuniting with a friend from 1980. This time I was more mature. My outlook on travel was more mature. I revisited the Grand Bazaar but I was interested in seeing so much more; The Hagia Sophia and the Blue Mosque, the Topkapi Palace and the Basilica Sistern. I wanted to sample all the food and learn about the culture. I was in love with Istanbul.

I returned in 2008 and was certain that I wanted to spend more time there. I subsequently started my English teaching career in Izmit and life was to get very colourful and unpredictable for me. Living and working in Izmit, I could visit Istanbul frequently as it was only a one hour bus journey away. I was able to revisit many sites and work my way through the numerous museums and galleries.

One of my favourite activities was to take a Bosphorus ferry cruise. I loved being on the water and motoring past the impressive mansions that lined the waterfront. Stopping off at Ortaköy to enjoy a delicious *kumpier*. This culinary delight consists of a huge, hot jacket potato cut in half. Its insides are mashed with butter and returned to the shell with a zillion other ingredients making it a monumental feast. My son and I would take the ferry to Ortaköy just to indulge in this treat. You could get them in other places, but here they were undoubtedly the best.

Istanbul has so many different suburbs and areas to explore that we never ran out of new adventures. Of course, first stop is always Sultanahmet, the historic heart of the city. Its where most of the famous tourist attractions are located. Its a frenetic mix of colour and sound; the call to prayer known as the *ezan*, echoing out of the Blue Mosque and other mosques five times a day against the back drop of manic traffic and car horns blaring.

Next, a stroll down to Eminönü where the various ferry boats leave or walk across the Galata Bridge that spans the Golden Horn and connects the two sides of Istanbul. Fishermen line the sides of the bridge and underneath are various seafood restaurants. You can indulge in a seafood feast or we always opted for a fish sandwich which cost a few lira and was delicious.

Then there is Beyoğlu and the Galata Tower, Taksim and the famous Istiklal Caddesi where the iconic red tram runs the length of this hectic pedestrian way; loaded with atmosphere and colour, people and restaurants, gorgeous architecture and astounding history.

One weekend in 2015, my friend suggested a drive to one of his favourite seafood restaurants in Sariyer. This district is one of Istanbul's most northern suburbs on the Black Sea. Its well known for its fresh fish and the little port is teeming with colourful fishing boats and piles of fishing nets. It all sounded lovely and I was keen to explore somewhere new.

This was a monumental mistake. The journey from Bakırköy to Sariyer should take around thirty minutes. Instead, we were sat in traffic for almost three hours. Obviously, being the weekend, everyone had the same idea as us. There was no other obvious reason for the holdup. Whilst my friend sat behind the wheel in bumper to bumper traffic, I was able to run across to a roadside restaurant, use the bathroom, order a snack and a drink for us and return to the car before he had even moved an inch. Yes, this wasn't the first time I had experienced horrendous traffic in Istanbul. The moral of this story is that unless you are born and raised in Istanbul with a high tolerance level for traffic stress, don't even think about driving.

Another weekend mistake on my part, was a visit to the Princes' Islands, Kizil Adalar. This small group of islands in the middle of the Sea of Marmara had been recommended to me as an escape from the chaos and madness of Istanbul. Even websites that I researched said that due to the absence of all vehicles, the only sound you will hear is silence. Now, I was wanting some of that.

All my information was wrong. I should have realized as I waited for the ferry to Büyükada, the largest of the Princes' Islands. The throbbing crowd were pushing and shoving in an effort to get on the ferry first. That's because of the limited seating on board and I ended up standing for the entire forty five minute journey. Then when we arrived, it was another frenzied mash of people fighting to be first off the boat.

Boasting no motorized vehicles but only bicycles and horse drawn carriages, I soon realized the reason for the race. The race was on to get a bicycle and the roads soon became a chaotic collage of wheels and handlebars vying for their room on the road. Bike horns were honking, novice riders were wobbling and there seemed to be no order to the cycling madness.

The idea of a ride on a horse drawn carriage sounded romantic but the queue for this was never-ending and polite queuing isn't a characteristic often attributed to Turks. So, off I went on foot trying to avoid being run over by the cycling masses and waiting patiently for a gap to cross the street. The architecture was outstanding but I just needed a coffee and to be on the next ferry boat out of there. It certainly wasn't the peaceful paradise that I had been promised.

Oh Istanbul, I love you but after a few days, I'm so ready to leave you.

When I was living in Çanakkale, I would always travel to Istanbul to meet my visitors at the airport and we would always spend a few days there. I would book an exotic Ottoman hotel to impress them and they were always impressed. After check-in, its customary to be invited to partake in a beverage in the lavish hotel lounge. For my guests this was always a great introduction to Turkish hospitality. Then the traditional dressed porters would take their baggage and accompany them to their rooms. By the way, I'm not talking expensive five star hotels but more the classic boutique hotels in beautifully restored Ottoman houses.

Next we would take to the streets to explore the neighbourhood and I would proudly show them around. I was proud of Istanbul and Turkey as a whole. I had chosen to live in this country and I was a proud and loyal ambassador.

I'd started to learn where to eat and where to avoid. I was well experienced in all the scams and con artists that would approach and fortunately, I had never been a victim of these but knew many people who had been. Istanbul is no different from any other big city but maybe a bit more imaginative. Some of the scams I heard about were truly ingenious.

A young American lad that I had befriended at a youth hostel down south, had told me his unfortunate experience which had truly tainted his impression of Turkey as a whole and he couldn't wait to go home. He had been in the park in front of the Blue Mosque minding his own business and in awe of the mosque that he had just visited. Two young Turkish men had joined him on the bench and offered him a cigarette whilst starting up a conversation. They seemed friendly enough and as he was travelling alone, he was grateful for some company. They invited him out that evening and promised to show him a great time.

The evening came and true to their word, they were waiting for him. They took him to a night club and ordered drinks. Next, a group of young woman joined them and all was going well. It seemed to be a fun evening until the check came. This young American guy was forced to pay the grossly over- charged bill for everyone. Because he didn't have that much cash on him, they bashed him up and took him to an ATM and waited whilst he emptied his account to his limit. Afraid that they would return the next day for more cash, he shuffled off into the dark, leaving his hostel and continuing on his way.

Carpet sellers are infamous for pressuring their customers into buying their wares. They are friendly and welcoming, offering a cup of apple tea as they roll out numerous rugs before the unsuspecting victim and deliver their well rehearsed spiel. At that point, its difficult to walk out of the shop empty handed. Sadly, its not unheard of for cheap China rugs to be sold as authentic Turkish carpets. Yes, even with a certificate of authenticity.

Istanbul isn't for the fainthearted. You have to keep your wits about you at every moment, every purchase, every taxi ride and every seemingly, friendly encounter. But at the end of the day, Istanbul is an awesome city that will never fail to enchant and excite.

The kindness of strangers

When it comes to hospitality and generosity, I think my experiences in Turkey definitely outshine any other place I've travelled or lived. In considering my own country, which is generally a very friendly and kind country, I have to ask; would we invite a perfect stranger into our home and make them feel so welcome?

I took a flight from Istanbul to Izmir. I wanted to go and visit the ancient Greek city of Ephesus. My plan was to stay the night in Izmir and then bus it to the closest town of Selçuk and visit Ephesus the next day.

I boarded the plane and was seated next to a young Turkish man dressed quite formally in a suit and tie and reading through a mountain of papers. He looked very official. I said '*merhaba*' as I took my seat and proceeded to get comfortable for the one hour flight to Izmir. It was late afternoon and I hadn't made a hotel reservation but I didn't have any doubt that I would find one easy enough.

"*Merhaba*," he replied. "Where are you from?"

I get that so much that it really does become old very fast but I always try to be friendly and courteous. I do understand the fascination and I do understand that a woman traveling solo in Turkey isn't the norm and is likely to arouse some interest.

"I'm from Australia," I replied. "How about you?"

"I'm a Turk," he replied proudly.

"Yes, I gathered that but from which city?" I continued.

"I'm from a city called Kuşadası. Do you know it?" he asked.

At this early stage of my Turkish life I wasn't aware of the city Kuşadası but he explained that it was a coastal town not far from Izmir and he was returning home after working the week in Istanbul. He was a young lawyer, recently married and living with his wife and her mother.

"Your English is very good," I remarked. "I'm an English teacher in Izmit."

He explained how he had studied English since he was a child and realized the importance of it for his career.

"My name is Ali," he introduced himself.

"*Memnun oldum*," I replied. "My name is Matilda."

"Oh, you speak Turkish," he commented with a beaming smile.

"No, just a few phrases really," I replied. "But I do try and use them when I can."

We chatted on and I explained to Ali my plans for my weekend. How excited I was to visit Ephesus and that it was a dream come true to be visiting these famous archaeological sites. He was excited for me and eager to share his knowledge about the area.

"You know Kuşadası is also close to Ephesus?" he told me. "It is a beautiful city that you should also visit."

I confessed that I hadn't ever heard of it but was open to all suggestions and that's how I liked to travel. I loved to be spontaneous and follow up on excellent recommendations.

"Thank you," I replied. "I might check it out."

Our hour of conversation had gone so fast and without even realizing it, our plane was landing at Izmir airport and my adventure was about to begin.

Everyone was in the aisle, readying for disembarkation. Phones were dinging and ringing. My friendly lawyer was also on his phone, no doubt to his wife, announcing his arrival. I was about to leave my seat and join the queue when Ali said something that completely blew me away. I didn't know how to respond. I was so humbled and filled with gratitude.

"You know, my wife is picking me up at the airport," he said. "We would be greatly honoured if you would join us this night."

"Hmm, wow, that's such a kind offer but perhaps your wife has other plans," I replied.

"No, No. I just checked with her and she has made the offer. She and her mother will cook for us and we offer you our spare room for the night."

This was beyond any gesture of kindness and hospitality that I had ever received and it was the first of many during my time living in Turkey.

"Wow, that is so generous of you," I replied. "I am a complete stranger to you."

"We welcome you into our family and our home," he continued.

Things were going through my mind as the suspicious westerner that I was but every stupid thought was trumped by feelings of gratitude. As I traveller, I was well aware that these special moments can never be planned and to jump at opportunities like this; to be spontaneous and trust in the powers of intuition and hope. I had felt completely at ease with this young man and my gut feeling was to go for it.

"I would be honoured to meet your family and accept your very generous offer," I replied.

I could see on Ali's face just how happy he was that I had accepted. I was a lucky woman, for sure.

Ali's family were amazing. Some of their cousins also visited so as to meet me. I felt like a celebrity. I was seated at the head of the table and a magnificent feast was laid on for me, his wife and her mother had been slaving away in the kitchen. It was a most enjoyable evening and one that I will never forget.

The next day Ali's wife left early for work. She worked at the Starbucks café on the pier. Ali, his mother-in-law and I went to visit her. We sat at the tables outside looking over to a small island called Pigeon Island that we would later visit. We were treated to coffee and muffins whilst we soaked in a bit of sunshine on the jetty.

We spent the morning exploring Kuşadası and then later that afternoon I was taken to the bus station and put on the bus for Selçuk. I didn't leave empty handed though. Along with my colourful memories, I took a kilo of Starbucks coffee, a couple of muffins for the road and a beautifully hand knitted scarf from Ali's mother-in-law.

What a brilliant detour I had experienced and I had made some wonderful new friends.

When I think back to that encounter, I am always reminded of how important it is to be trusting, to be open to offers of kindness, to say 'yes' to unexpected opportunities and how to always be gracious and grateful. Also, just a few words of the local language can open many doors and take you through the gateway into a new culture.

Paragliding off Babadağ

I think many women feel this way after divorce. Well, some of us. I felt like a giant weight had been lifted from my shoulders and I was free, unshackled and liberated. I was bold, brave and intrepid, in search of adventure and new experiences. I wanted to feel the rush of excitement again. I wanted to go paragliding.

Babadağ is a mountain near Fethiye on the Mediterranean coast. It is approximately two thousand metres high and its where they paraglide. I decided that this would be my next intrepid venture. I had already gone hot air ballooning and this seemed like the next obvious progression to get that high that I was seeking.

That was in 2009. Looking back, I don't know if I would have the same courage today. I would probably find enough reasons not to and be happy enough to watch them flying from a beach side cafe. I've since heard of numerous accidents at Oludeniz and I wasn't keen to let my son fly a few years later. But back in 2009, I was in a much different mindset.

It was April and the weather was glorious. Blue skies and a perfect temperature. Maybe, a little cool in the evenings but that's how I like it. I travelled down to Fethiye and stayed at a fun and lively hostel where I met two young Australian lads who also had their heart set on paragliding. Together we travelled the short distance to Oludeniz which was where all the action was happening.

As soon as we got off the bus, vendors from the various paragliding companies approached us, offering their brochures and 'special' prices. The season was just starting and so the number of customers was still slim. We could negotiate an acceptable price for the three of us. After all the paper work was done, there was nothing to do but wait for the call.

It had been a clear blue sky day but the wind had been a bit stronger than desired and so we had to wait a couple hours for the conditions to improve. Probably around sunset, they had told us.

So, of course, we headed to a cafe and enjoyed the afternoon with a beer or two. One of our trio didn't quite think it through and he had indulged in more than one or two beers. By the time our call came he was quite inebriated. I wouldn't have liked to have been in his shoes.

There was about ten of us now and we all climbed into the back of a red 4WD truck. It would take us up the rugged dirt road to the top of the mountain. We took our seats, five of us on each side of the truck and watched the stunning scenery as we slowly drove higher and higher. There was nervous chatter and everyone was excited.

When we finally arrived at the summit, the Turkish crew were busy unpacking the kits and getting the gear organized, whilst we were all suited up and given helmets. The Australian guy with too much beer in his gut had offloaded some of it after the steep and bumpy drive up the mountain. He didn't look good.

This was getting real now as we watched as the kites were

positioned in readiness for flight. The organization had been top notch and it was almost launch time. Still time to back out, I thought. No, this was something I really needed to do and I was ready.

We each wore a harness that was connected to our tandem pilot. All of the pilots were so handsome, so that was a bonus. I was instructed to shuffle into place and we watched whilst the first gliders took off, waiting nervously for our turn. I was lost in a trance. It was mesmerizing. Then it was our turn.

"Run," my pilot called. "Run."

The ground below my feet was rocky and slippery as I obediently ran towards the edge. I don't know what I was thinking at that time. It all happened so fast. I was in the zone. Before I knew it, we were airborne, soaring above the mountain below us, looking down at the cliff from which we had just jumped. The wind in our sail taking us higher and higher. It was exhilarating. The views below my feet were breathtaking.

The timing couldn't have been more ideal. The sun was starting to set and the golden glow on the landscape below us was stunning. The silence and serenity added to the almost religious experience. Fellow para-gliders were dancing and circling above and below us, silhouetted against the sky.

For almost forty minutes we circled and soared like a bird. We dipped and rose again going where the wind took us and I guess where my pilot steered us. We looked down on the beach at Oludeniz and saw people as ants on the beach. Flying over rooftops and slowly losing altitude, I realized that we were going in for our landing.

I videoed the whole landing as we approached the beach and crew members were there to catch us and it was that easy. In my mind, I had pictured a much faster and abrupt landing but it wasn't to be. With the help of the crew we landed rather gracefully. It was over but the high stayed with us for some time. It had been an epic experience for me and one I will never forget.

Would I do it again? I think I would. Maybe.

A Sunday feast out east

Doğubayazıt is a small city in the easternmost region of Turkey on the border with Iran. It is a pit stop on the legendary Silk Road and it had been on my wish list for quite a while. In October of 2014 I found the opportunity to make this journey and it was everything I hoped it would be. There is so much about this region that fascinates me and I know that it always will.

The magnificent Mt Ararat is a mere fifteen kilometres away and many adventure junkies come here to climb Turkey's highest peak. There is a striking rock formation that is believed to be the wreck of Nuh'un Ambari, better known as Noah's Ark. The BBC and Joanna Lumley made a brilliant documentary out here and it is well worth watching. There is also a massive meteor crater, Meteor Çukuru, which lies just a few kilometres from the Iranian border. From this point one can see the massive convoy of cargo trucks waiting to get their permission to cross over the border. I've heard that the trucks could be queued up there for over a week. I didn't see any wash room facilities; those poor truck drivers.

But the biggest attraction for me lay just south of the city. I had come to explore the glorious İşak Paşa Sarayı or better known as the

Ishak Pasha Palace. Strategically perched on a rocky hill overlooking the sand coloured barren plains of Kurdistan, this mighty Ottoman palace is a photographer's dream.

Decorative arches and domes, windswept courtyards and intricate wall carvings all add to the opulence and grandeur of this now deserted and forgotten palace. When I was there a new bride was having her photos taken against the romantic backdrop. I can only imagine how beautiful those photos must have turned out.

It was a Sunday and the minibus that brought me here was packed with families and their picnics. They weren't interested in visiting the palace. It was just there. It had always been there. They were all heading up the hill to a large dusty picnic area where they would enjoy their afternoon with friends and family. And so, after my rambling through the palace ruins, I decided to head up to the picnic area to observe the activity. There was plenty to observe.

In one area of the park, a family was celebrating the circumcision of their son. The *sünnet* is an important part of Turkish culture, a rite of passage and defines the moment when a boy becomes a man. I don't know when the poor little boy had faced the knife but it was obvious that a goat had been recently slaughtered in his honour as the skin and entrails hung from a tree and the greedy flies buzzed incessantly. A banquet had been prepared and the men were busily organizing the grill whilst the women set the table and attended to the children. There was plenty of laughter and merriment and the music was blaring from a black dusty CD player resting in a fork of a tree.

I kept walking and came upon a cluster of small makeshift stalls that had been set up to sell colourful plastic toys from China as well as sweets and soft drinks. The park lacked any grass but the families were happy to set up on the dirt sitting on large tarps and rugs. Wearing loose baggy pants, colourful blouses and headscarves, the women sat cross-legged on the ground chopping, cutting and preparing the foods for the feast. To the side was the obligatory pot of Turkish tea brewing.

Joy and happiness was in the air and one is reminded that wherever you are in the world, the family, children and friends are the fundamentals of life. Australian, English, Turkish or Kurd, we all love our children. Preparing and sharing a meal together whilst the children are playing is universal.

I was the stranger there but I received many welcoming waves and gestures. I guess there was some intrigue as to why I was here because this place wasn't really on any tourist trail and I was probably the only foreigner in the park. One large family group gestured me over to share a glass of tea with them. I was honoured and took a place on the ground amongst them. My elementary Turkish was enough for us to be able to hold a simple conversation and they were delighted at my efforts. The younger children were crawling all over me whilst the mother continued to knead and mould the *köfte,* Turkish meat balls in her hands. The teenage daughter, dressed similar to her mother, was washing the green leaves for the salad and serving the tea.

The father was happily squatting whilst tending to the fire and chatting with me. A large batch of chicken pieces was already cooking upon the grill and the smell was intoxicating. Next, he placed the *köfte* alongside the chicken and the husband and wife exchanged some dialogue regarding the preparation of their lunch. In all of Turkey, food is a very important part of life and they certainly know how to prepare a grand feast. I had brought no food with me and my stomach was now growling for what was before me.

The mother went to the boxes and bags and brought out tomatoes, spring onions and large round flat bread which she placed in the centre of the rug. She tore a piece of the flat bread and placed a spring onion and some green leafs upon it. She had her husband place a chicken piece upon that and folded it together and offered it to me. How could I refuse? My taste buds were dancing as I munched into this delectable chicken wrap. I hadn't realized how hungry I was but now there was no stopping me. Everyone happily feasted and the children sat in their place whilst the mother served them their lunch. There was no place for my shyness as this kind family continued to see that my plate was full.

After a long and delicious feast, the father gave the children some money to go to the stalls and buy a toy. Like children all over the world they squealed wildly, running off with the five lira note in their hands. I decided to join them and together we looked at all the plastic junk on sale from which they each selected a toy. I bought some soft drinks and sweets and we returned to the family picnic. The father was now lying down dozing in the late afternoon sun. The mother and daughter were cleaning up and packing up and once again we enjoyed a glass of tea.

I needed to use the bathroom and the mother directed me down the hill to a small concrete building that had written on it in bright green paint the letters W.C. As I approached the smell was overwhelming and I knew that I couldn't continue. Since I had been travelling in the east, it had become an obsession of mine to find a decent clean toilet and I usually preferred to find a bush. In this case, with so many people around, a private bush in a sandy and barren park was impossible to find. I just had to hold my nose and do a quick squat inside this pit of filth.

Despite this bathroom experience, it had been an amazing day. I was so grateful to my new friends for their wonderful hospitality. The sun was starting to set and the sky was a brilliant shade of pink, which highlighted the palace again and the endless plains of sand and rock. My family were now getting ready to go home and I helped them with their bags as we walked down the dusty path to their big blue tractor. Loading everything into the trailer, the mother and all the kids happily piled in as well. The father started up the engine and the tractor pulled out onto the road.

I stood there watching them as they slowly made their way down the hill and home. All the while, that wonderful family filled with smiles and happiness waved me goodbye as they bounced along in the trailer.

As I waited for the minibus to take me back to town, I had a final look around at where I was. I was filled with gratitude that I had had the opportunity to visit this amazing place and to experience the hospitality and friendship of these wonderful people. It really was the most special memory for me from that trip out east. The hospitality and friendship that I encountered was truly humbling and I often wonder if we in the west would be as welcoming and generous to perfect strangers.

The best bus trip ever

The rain was pelting down and my trip down the mountain in the local *marshrutka* had been a hair-raising experience. There had been numerous rock slides and at one point a massive boulder had fallen from the cliff above and blocked our way. The rain was torrential with gushing streams running either side of this small treacherous road. We were delayed for quite a while, whilst efforts were made to move the boulder and let the traffic continue on its way.

Our driver was obviously frustrated and very edgy, yelling and screaming and talking to himself. It was quite a terrifying time for us passengers but all we could do was sit tight and hope that we weren't going to be swept away.

I had been on a three week adventure to explore the Republic of Georgia, a fascinating and amazingly scenic country that lay to the north east of Turkey. Most of my trip had been marred by rain but I'd managed to get three days of sunny blue skies in Mestia, in the Upper Svaneti. It had been the highlight of my trip and I had enjoyed hiking in the fresh mountain air.

Now I was heading home. From my hostel it was a rather daunting hundred and thirty kilometre trip down the mountain to the town of Zugdidi where I could catch a regular bus to Batumi on the Black Sea. From Batumi I could then cross over the border back into Turkey. As much as I had enjoyed this adventure, I was exhausted as travelling by these *marshrutkas* wasn't for the faint-hearted. They were terribly uncomfortable, usually packed to capacity, and I had yet to meet a friendly driver. Not to mention that in Georgia, a former Soviet country, the roads were horrendous with giant potholes and all sorts of domestic animals wandering aimlessly along them. Many times we had screeched to a halt for a stray cow or pig.

I had left my hostel in Mestia at seven thirty in the morning and now it was twelve thirty and we were still stuck on the mountain with the rain beating heavily against the side of our vehicle. There was nothing to do but be patient and positive but by this stage I was definitely ready to go home.

Finally we pushed on through the driving rain and arriving in Zugdidi, I was lucky to catch a bus straight to Batumi. The rain hadn't let up and the main street of Batumi was flooded. The bus just dropped me off somewhere near the centre of town. The driver had yelled to me that this was my stop and so I gathered my stuff and stepped off into a flowing torrent of water. My shoes and lower legs were instantly soaked.

I needed to get my bearings and try and find some cover but he had dropped me near a large park and I needed to run through manic traffic and massive puddles to get over to the shops. Within minutes I was drenched. The rain was pouring down my face, my hair was completely saturated and my glasses were so foggy I couldn't even see where I was running. The traffic wouldn't ease up to let me cross and I just surrendered to my situation and considered that I'd rather be wet than run over.

Really, I was ready to go home. So ready. I was soaked to the bone and feeling drained of all energy. Eventually, I found my way to the bus ticket office and looking more like a drowned river rat, I entered the office to enquire about the next bus across the border to Trabzon in Turkey.

The bus office was for a company called Golden Buses and the girl sitting behind the counter, warm and dry, just looked at me with distaste.

"Auto bus Trabzon?" I asked.

She was Georgian but lucky for me she also spoke Turkish. She showed me the timetable and the next bus was leaving in two hours' time and would pick me up here at the office. I was so relieved. I was going home. I hadn't heard of this particular bus company before but she assured me that it was a Turkish company. Thank God.

Now I could sit back and relax but I soon became aware that I was shivering incessantly. I mean I was frozen to the bone. I needed to dry off and change my clothes. Unfortunately I only had the one pair of shoes with me and they made squishing sounds as I walked.

"*Havlu lütfen?*" I asked politely hoping she might have a towel out the back.

She looked at me coldly and offered me the tissue box. At least I could dry my glasses.

Most of clothes in my bag were also wet by this stage but I managed to find a couple of dry if not dirty items. I needed to get out of my wet pants. Even my underwear was soaked. Again, I troubled this poor girl, as I asked if I could use the bathroom. I could see a storeroom and bathroom at the back of her office behind where she sat.

"*Banyo, lütfen?*"

She looked so coldly upon me and shook her head from side to side.

"No" she answered.

Well then, I would just change my clothes there in the office. I proceeded to take off my shoes and socks and was about to unzip my pants when she called out to me.

"Tamam, tamam."

Angrily she led me out the back to the office bathroom.

I was very grateful but couldn't understand why she was so resistant to being kind. I mean what was the harm? Throughout my travels in Georgia I had met some wonderful and hospitable people. In Tblisi I had met Bahman, a professor at the University of Georgia and he had gone out of his way to show me his beautiful city. He even took me on a tour of the University and I got to sit in on one of his lectures which were all given in English. In Mestia I had met lots of kind and friendly locals. Though the bus drivers were always quite scary and aggressive, my fellow passengers had always been friendly and kind. One lady had even invited me to her home for a lunch with her family. So why was this girl so cold and unsympathetic? Surely, she could see my predicament.

"Tesekkur ederim."

I thanked her as I returned to the office waiting room feeling slightly drier but still shivering.

Tissues hadn't really helped and my hair was still quite wet but at least I had dry clothes on now and I was grateful for that. I just sat and tried to relax whilst I waited for my bus to arrive.

Finally, the bus pulled into the curb. Yes, I was ready to go.

As I climbed aboard the bus I was warmly welcomed by the

driver and his assistant. So far I was the only passenger and they were happy to give me all of their attention. They were so friendly and kind and I felt that warm sense of home.

I found my seat near the back of the bus and tried to get comfortable but I was so cold. I was cold on the inside and couldn't help shivering. The young *garson*, the one who usually serves the coffees and teas approached me. He wanted to make the usual small talk in English.

"Where you from?" he asked.

"I'm from Australia." I replied.

"What you do?" he continued.

"I've just had a holiday in Georgia. I live in Turkey. I'm an English teacher," I replied, not sure how much information he wanted.

"Oh, my *hoca*. Are you cold? You shaking," he asked.

"Yes, I am very cold. I was caught in the rain and all my clothes got wet," I replied.

As well as cold, I was starting to feel extremely sleepy. It had been a long day and the feeling of going home was comforting and I was finally able to relax.

"One minute, my *hoca*," he said as he returned to the front of the bus. We were obviously waiting for another passenger to arrive and the bus's engine was turned off.

Immediately he turned the key and the motor revved into action and so did the heater. Within no time, I could feel the warmth of the heater coming through the vent at my feet. It was glorious. If that wasn't enough, he then brought me a blanket and tucked me in. Yes, it was only a Turkish bus but I felt like I was already was back in Turkey.

Eventually we pulled out to begin our journey home. At the border I had to get off to show my documents but the kind *garson* lead me all the way and then back to the waiting bus on the Turkish side. There was a short delay there, as they were obviously stocking up on the duty free alcohol and cigarettes. If I had had the energy I would have also stocked up on some alcohol and maybe some cigarettes for my friend back home, but what the heck, I just couldn't be bothered. I was so tired.

Finally, we were on the road to Trabzon. No more disruptions. I could relax, listen to my music and chill, even get some sleep as it was about a three-hour journey and we would be arriving quite late. I'd need some more energy to find a hotel for the night.

There were only two staff and three passengers on the bus. It was quiet and peaceful.

"My *hoca*, are you warm?" my wonderful *garson* asked.

"Yes, thank you. The heater and blanket are very good. You are very kind," I replied in simple English.

He smiled and left, happy for my words.

He soon returned with a paper cup in his hand and a small packet of cheese crackers.

"You like?" he asked as he offered me the cup.

Thinking it was coffee, I gladly accepted his offering. The intense aroma teased my senses and I soon realized that it wasn't coffee. It was a cup full of whiskey. Oh my God. That was exactly what I needed!

I was so grateful I didn't have enough words to express my appreciation but I think he got it.

"*Çok teşekkür ederim*", I replied.

I was really so overwhelmed with gratitude and so happy to be back in Turkey.

When we arrived at the Trabzon bus station it was quite late. My wonderful *garson* wasn't going to desert me now. He called around and found me a hotel room. He insisted I eat with him and the bus driver at the bus station cafeteria and he wouldn't allow me to pay. Then he put me in a taxi and instructed the driver to take me to my hotel.

Oh Turkey, I was so happy to be home and really, that was the best bus trip ever.

My hitch-hiking adventures

Hitch-hiking, for those who are not familiar, is a form of transport in which one stands along the roadside or in a petrol station with their thumb up in the hope of scoring a free ride with a passing motorist. It can be intimidating and scary until you get used to it. It can be dangerous too but it can also be fun and a wonderful way to meet the locals. Of course, the benefits are that it saves you money, can be a lot more comfortable than the public transport and considering you get a ride straight away, it's usually much faster.

My first hitch-hiking experiences were in Europe in the 1980s. We were budget conscious backpackers looking for adventure and hitch-hiking provided that sense of intrepidity and comfort. It was fun and we met nice people and often our experience lead to us being offered a meal along the way. I never hitched alone and as two young girls we never had any problems stopping motorists for a ride and fortunately most of our experienced were positive and we lived to ride another day.

When I began living in Turkey, hitch-hiking once again became one of my travel options. In Turkey they call it 'auto stopping'.

After a year of living in the bustling industrial city of Izmit, I moved to the smaller provincial town of Çanakkale. Çanakkale lies on the Dardanelles Straits in north-western Turkey and is just a ferryboat hop away from the World War One battle fields of Gallipoli. It is a city surrounded by glorious nature and fascinating history. I loved living there and stayed for over five years.

Across the Dardanelles on the European side were many magical nature places to explore. The long stretch of beach at Anzac Cove was a delight to stroll any time of year and in summer the water was warm and crystal clear. Knowing the local history added a special feeling of privilege at being able to enjoy this area. My friend had a motorbike and we would often explore further afield and find small deserted coves and little fishing villages.

With living in the noisy city centre and teaching English, I often craved the silence and solitude of the beaches of Saros Gulf. If my friend was working, getting there without transport was a bit of a problem. I would have to take the ferryboat across the straits and then there was only one bus to take me to Saros Gulf. It was at three o'clock in the afternoon to connect with the larger ferryboat taking passengers to Gökçeada, one of the Turkish islands. In summer this service was, of course, more frequent but that didn't help me during the off-season months.

I would pack myself a picnic, gather my writing and reading materials into my small backpack and take the ferryboat across to the town of Eceabat on the European side. There I would walk out of town until I was on the main road and put up my thumb. Yes, at fifty three years old, I was once more on the road hitch-hiking. I never ever had a problem getting a ride. Often, I could even score a ride on the ferryboat as it was a car ferry and most traffic was heading to

Istanbul and therefore going my way. A few kilometres out of town, is the Anzac Cove turn-off. They could just drop me there and I could find a new ride for the remaining eight kilometres but more often than not, they drove me the entire way. I found that most of my lifts were courteous and intrigued. They had stumbled upon this Australian woman in the middle of nowhere and were eager to hear my story or practice their English. If they spoke no English at all, they were excited to hear my most basic Turkish.

On one such adventure, I was coming back from Anzac Cove. It was a bit late in the day and I had started walking along the peaceful stretch of road that overlooks the Saros Gulf and out to Gökçeada. The sun was beginning to set and the sky was a soothing pink colour. I felt free and alive and didn't have a care in the world. I knew I would get a ride at some stage but I was enjoying my surrounds.

Before not too long a car passed slowly and then stopped. They reversed back to me and asked me directions on how to get to the Eceabat ferryboat terminal. They were a young married couple from Istanbul on their honeymoon, exploring this special corner of Turkey and as luck would have it, that was exactly where I was heading. We hit it off immediately and chatted all the way, became good friends and kept in contact for quite some time.

Another time I came across a young couple trying to reach the 'Abide', a famous and highly revered Turkish war memorial on the southern side of the peninsula. It was further than I needed to go but I agreed to join them and be their guide and we had a memorable afternoon together, before they too took the car ferry to Çanakkale and drove me home.

I had had many memorable rides to and from Anzac Cove and it always added a tinge of excitement to my day out. All my rides had been positive experiences and I had always felt completely safe and looked after. In my youth, hitch-hiking had been more about saving the cost of a bus ticket, but at this stage of my life it was more about convenience and adventure.

It was March and I decided on a trip down the coast to the region of Antalya. I always prefer to travel out of season as the crowds during summer are unbearable to me and also I usually visit family and friends in Australia in the northern summer months.

I had travelled by bus all the way down the coast to the pretty Mediterranean seaside town of Kaş. However, my objectives for this adventure were to visit and enjoy some days in the smaller villages of Olympos and Çıralı. The bus from Kaş only went so far along the main road as it was off season and so I thought once more to try my hand at hitching a ride. As luck would have it, a scored a ride within no time and even received an English teaching job offer.

My time spent at both these villages was glorious. I had the most breath-taking beaches practically to myself. I stayed at the Saban Tree Houses and savoured the most authentic Turkish cuisine. It was a wonderful week of peace and relaxation exploring the area and just chilling.

I hitched back to the main road easily and perhaps slightly overconfident, I decided to try to hitch a ride back to Kaş. In fact, I even considered seeing just how far I could get on my travels home. My first ride was most successful: a business man doing his rounds and he was able to drop me on the main road just past the Kaş turn-off. He had been so kind and we had shared some interesting conversation and so I was on a hitch-hiker's high. I would try my luck again.

Strolling along the main road in the direction of Fethiye, it wasn't long before a car pulled in beside me and motioned for me to hop in. In the front seat was the driver, a young man that didn't look much older than eighteen and in the passenger seat was his elderly grandmother or perhaps great grandmother. She gave me a toothless smile as she clutched on to her cargo of vegetables and herbs.

I climbed into the back seat and explained that I was heading to Fethiye. He explained that he was driving his *büyükanne*, grandmother home and then continuing on to Fethiye. I welcomed the short detour to their home and saw how the family were outside waiting to welcome her and enthusiastically helped her with her bags of goodies. You don't experience that on the bus.

After a cool drink and some hearty conversation, everyone happily waved us off as we continued the drive to Fethiye with me now sitting in the front passenger's seat. All was going well, the sun was shining, the sky was blue and I felt at peace. Conversation was minimal but then out of the blue came what I could never have expected.

"*Seks?*" he muttered.

"What?" I exclaimed.

"*Seks?*" he repeated.

I couldn't help myself but I burst into laughter. Here was this young boy propositioning me and he didn't look too pleased at my laughter. Despite all the moral ramifications, it was still humourous to me to think that this young guy would want sex with a woman in her fifties. Also, I could see that this could have been a dangerous situation if it had been a fully grown male instead of this spindly light weight teenager.

"Stop the car here," I requested in my simple Turkish. "*Durmak!*"

Slowly and reluctantly he pulled over to the roadside. I grabbed my pack, slammed the door and started walking. Driving slowly alongside me, he pleaded with me to reconsider his 'offer'.

"Lütfen," he pleaded from his rolling vehicle. "Pleee.....ase,"

After accompanying me slowly down the road for a couple hundred metres, he finally got the message and zoomed off. I was still on the main road but in the middle of nowhere. I tried to hail down a large intercity coach but it just flashed its lights at me and zoomed by. I had no alternative now but to find another ride to the nearest bus station.

Luckily, my next ride soon appeared in the shape of a small weary truck bearing cases of vegetables. The driver seemed friendly enough and so I happily climbed aboard, relieved that I would soon be in Fethiye where I would definitely take the bus for the remainder of my journey.

It wasn't long before that small three letter word (four letters in Turkish) once more popped into the conversation and once more I demanded to be dropped off on the side of the road. I might be a slow learner but I really didn't feel comfortable taking any more rides this day and made the slow and weary walk into the next town and took a minibus to the Fethiye bus station where I could get a bus for home.

On reflection, of course, I can see how lucky I had been. I had put myself in a very vulnerable and potentially dangerous position and had been very fortunate in that I had returned home unscathed and had lived to share my experience and story.

After further consideration and thought, I also realized that down that part of Turkey, they do get a high volume of tourists and single women looking for a fling or holiday romance and so without justifying it, I think there is a different attitude to foreign women than up north where I lived. But when all is said and done, it had been foolish of me to even consider hitch-hiking in that part of Turkey.

On finally arriving home safely by bus, I was soon chastised by my friend and alerted of the story of the young Italian women who had been hitch-hiking from Milan to Turkey and had been raped and murdered before being found under the bushes in an area just outside of Istanbul. Hmmm....that was a chilling reminder of how lucky I had been.

I can't say I never took another ride to Anzac Cove, but I certainly didn't entertain the idea of auto-stopping further afield again.

Picnic at the lake

I was on one of my many expeditions to discover and explore different areas of Turkey. I had been in Antalya and then travelled inland to the Isparta Province and the peaceful Lake Eğirdir. It had been recommended to me and I was eager to check it out.

The pension that I had booked was well located next to the lake and my room had stunning views and captured an amazing sunset each evening. It was small and friendly and I loved having breakfast looking out over the lake with its fishing boats and picturesque harbour.

There is a small island, Yeşil Ada which is connected by a causeway and made for a pleasant stroll. On the island there is lush green parkland with barbecues and picnic tables. It was the weekend and the park was full of families picnicking and enjoying the perfect spring weather.

I was minding my own business and soaking up the atmosphere when I was suddenly set upon by a gaggle of excitable Turkish university students from the local Isparta University. Eğirdir is quite off the regular tourist trail so I guess I was probably the only foreigner there and I stood out like a sore thumb.

They were eager to practice their English with me and their enthusiasm and energy was refreshing. I was more than happy to chat with them and answer all their questions; 'Where are you from?' followed by 'Do you like Turkey?' and "What are you doing here?' and of course 'How old are you?'

It isn't the first time I have been questioned about my life. In Turkey it seems that it's perfectly acceptable to ask about one's age, marital status, how many children and even about my earnings. Nothing is off limits, it seems.

Firstly, I got an "Ahh we are sorry for you, *hoca*" when I told them I was divorced. They seemed to instantly feel so sad for me. I had to reassure them that I was perfectly happy on my own and fully capable of looking after myself. They couldn't comprehend a woman travelling alone in a foreign land. It seemed a concept that they just couldn't grasp.

Next they were interested in my opinion of their country. They were excited to hear me share my thoughts and excited that I loved living in their country. Yes, I love the food. Yes, I've tried *manti,* a kind of Turkish dumpling that seemed to be a big hit with all students. Of course, I love *baklava* and *kunefe,* two deliciously sweet desserts.

"Which country is the best, Australia or Turkey?"

I always needed to answer this one carefully and diplomatically.

"Both are beautiful," I would say. "It's hard for me to choose."

This day they were out on a social picnic day and they eagerly invited me to join them. I was honoured and grateful to be included in this happy group. It was fun. Whilst some of the students were preparing the barbecue which smelt absolutely divine, music was playing on a small radio that sat upon the picnic table. The rest of the students were dancing and singing. Before I knew it I was also dancing, rather reluctantly I might add. Though my dancing was not up to their abilities I still had a good laugh. A couple of the girls showed off their belly dancing skills whilst I recorded them on my camera. We took many photos together to remember this special day.

After a delicious lunch of barbecued chicken and salad, the students proceeded to play skipping rope, laughing and giggling like innocent little children. In my mind, I was thinking about the university students back in Australia. It certainly wouldn't be a picnic without alcohol and no one would be dancing without alcohol. I'm quite sure they wouldn't be playing skipping rope, maybe a game of cricket I thought. I was just observing and I guess comparing but it was an uplifting experience to be included in their company. We stayed friends for quite a while and I got some of them Australian contacts to practice their English with.

A couple of years later when I was teaching English in Çanakkale, I was invited to an end of semester party at the student residence of the local University. I was eager to attend. There was food and a DJ. The music was pumping, mostly Turkish pop. Once again I noticed the total absence of alcohol. These were university students celebrating the end of the year and partying to the full without the need of any stimulants. Again, I was pulled up to dance and again I was quite reluctant to do so as I realized that even I need a small boost of confidence from alcohol to hit the dance floor.

For those of you who may say that Turkey is an Islamic country and alcohol is forbidden, you would be wrong. Although certainly an Islamic country, Turkey is a secular society and alcohol is allowed. In regards to their religion, I was often told that it is between the individual and their God as to whether they drank or smoked, or participated in fasting during Ramazan.

Also, in some sectors of the society alcohol was a huge problem and I knew many an alcoholic whilst I lived there. But it was refreshing to see these fresh bright students partying without the need of any alcohol and I respected them for that.....though I really could have done with a glass of wine.

Balloons and fairy chimneys

When I first visited Turkey in 1985, it was on the back of a motorbike with my ex-husband. We came in through Thessaloniki and followed the coast down to Marmaris, where we took the car ferry to Rhodes. Along the way, I had seen many posters advertising Göreme in Cappadocia and to me, it looked captivating and I wanted desperately to go there. Unfortunately, my ex didn't share the same fascination and it remained an unfulfilled dream of mine until 2007.

If you've read my first book, *A Turkish Affair*, you will be familiar with my story. If not, here is a brief overview.

In 2006, with the modern technology that wasn't available to us in the early eighties, I was contacted by a Turkish boyfriend that I had first met in Greece in 1980. By 2007, twenty seven years after we had first met, we were sure we wanted to reunite in person. A plan was hatched and we rendezvoused in Istanbul and together we travelled to Cappadocia.

This long-held dream of mine was finally being realized. After all these years, I was going to Göreme. Yes, and it didn't disappoint. I'm sure that back in 1985, it was still a backwater waiting to be explored and only the most intrepid traveller made their way there. The phallic shaped fairy chimneys had been the main attraction back then and hiking in the enchanting valleys. Pictures of that strange alien landscape had been enough to seduce me.

That being said, in 2006 I could go hot air ballooning over that landscape and that was the most amazing experience. Again, if you've read *A Turkish Affair*, you'll know just how much I loved it. Its definitely a bucket list item.

Everything about Cappadocia made me smile. I was always happy there. During the six years that I lived in Turkey, I made four visits to Cappadocia and each time was fresh and new and exciting.

In 2009 I took my son. We were excited to go hot air ballooning together. I don't think he realized just how early you have to wake up. Having two sons, I was quite experienced with the fact that teenage boys don't like early mornings. Unfortunately for my son, most hot air ballooning happens at sunrise when the air temperature and wind conditions are optimal.

We purchased our tickets and had an early night. The hotel was going to give us a wake-up call which was a safety precaution in case I didn't wake up first. Of course, I woke up first and tried to stir my son. It took some effort. The mornings were quite cool by October and he was snug in his bed.

"Come on, sleepy head. Time to get up," I said.

He wasn't impressed.

"Come on, they'll be here soon to pick us up," I continued.

Reluctantly, he climbed out of his warm cocoon of blankets and got dressed but he was definitely still in zombie mode. I gently steered him to reception and we waited for the ride. Coffee would be necessary.

Our pickup was on-time and we headed out into the darkness to the launching site. When we arrived we were offered hot drinks and biscuits and I could see my son slowly come alive. We were surrounded by hot air balloons being inflated. There were so many of them. It was exhilarating. The colours of the surrounding landscape were beginning to change as the sun was slowly rising above the horizon. The many colours of the partially inflated balloons were a spectacle. The red hot burner flames lit up our surroundings and its still a mystery to me, how the balloons don't just dissolve into flames.

We were a small group of travellers from various countries bonding in anticipation of this once in a lifetime activity. The excitement was palpable. However, there had been some concern around the coffee table. The word was that the wind conditions were too strong and therefore launching couldn't go ahead. Sighs and gasps heralded everyone's disappointment. No, this can't be happening. Of course, we all wanted to be safe and we appreciated the safety concerns but this was major let down. Another coffee and we all waited patiently for the final word. Perhaps, if we waited thirty minutes the winds might calm down.

My son took the opportunity to explore the launching site and he took some of the most striking photos; photos of the sad looking half inflated balloons, photos of the sun rising against a rocky background.

Ultimately, a decision was made and for the safety of all involved, the flights were cancelled for the day. There was nothing to do but go and feed our sorrows with a massive Turkish breakfast. Luckily, we still had another day in Cappadocia and so we could try again tomorrow. The idea of another early morning wasn't so appealing but then again who knows if we'd ever be this way again.

Sadly, the next morning the conditions were the same and so my son never got to go hot air ballooning in Cappadocia. Still he experienced the landscape on foot and we have many beautiful memories from that time.

I had wanted to experience Cappadocia in the winter. I had wanted to see the snow upon the fairy chimneys. The Christmas of 2013, I made this a reality and again, was not disappointed. I flew into Nevşehir and arrived around midnight. I had organized a ticket on the shuttle bus to my cave hotel in Göreme. Whilst we waited for all the passengers to arrive, the temperature in Nevşehir at that time was a frosty minus eleven degrees Celsius. It was cold.

When I arrived at the cave hotel, I was greeted with a warming glass of sherry and shown to my cozy, warm room. I can say that whenever I'm in Cappadocia the hotels that I have chosen have always been wonderful and that's another reason Cappadocia is probably my all time favourite place to visit.

This trip I explored underground cities and Christian rock churches. I enjoyed the food and photographing the fairy chimneys covered in snow. What a wonderland. If you haven't been already, I highly recommend that you add it to your bucket list and prepare to be in awe of its beauty.

The creepiest museum in the world

On one of my trips to Cappadocia I had visited the small town of Avanos which is well known for its thousand year history of ceramics and pottery. A pleasant little town just 18 kilometres from Nevşehir and overlooking the Kızılırmak or Red River, I thought it would make for a nice day trip and lunch stop. I could never have believed what I was about to stumble upon.

Situated in one of the pottery shops was the creepiest museum that I had ever encountered. It was the Avanos Hair Museum. Yes, that's right, Hair Museum.

Curiosity got the better of me and I had to make a visit. The museum is inside a pottery store but once you go down the stairs it becomes really creepy. Hanging from all the walls and even the ceiling are locks of hair attached to the owner's name, address and phone number. I was told that only female hair is accepted but I had no desire to leave any of my curls there. It felt totally claustrophobic to me and I didn't want any of those locks of hair to touch me. I honestly couldn't wait to get out.

This little museum began its story nearly forty years ago and so you can imagine how many locks of hair are hanging there and even the day I visited, women were adding to the bizarre collection. Why? You might be asking this very question as I sure was.

Of course, there is a story, a legend, a tale. Who knows if it's true but probably it is because I can't think of any other reason for collecting hair samples; over 16,000 of them to date.

The story goes like this. A local potter, who was saying goodbye to his love, requested that she give him a lock of her hair to remember her by. He attached the hair to his wall as a constant reminder of her and he delighted in telling his customers the sad story.

Apparently, on hearing his sorrowful tale, other women were incited to leave him a lock of their hair with their contact details and sometimes even a photo. So since 1997 he has built up quite a collection and his small museum situated in the basement of his pottery shop is now listed in the Book of Guinness World records and is certainly one of the weirdest and creepiest tourist attractions I've ever visited.

Does visiting the Hair Museum appeal to you?

TURKISH DIARIES

2015

Time to move on

TURKISH DIARIES

Leaving Turkey

This story and the next, I wrote back in 2015 when I had decided that the time had come to move on and leave Turkey. It wasn't an easy decision and it certainly wasn't an easy trip either. It felt like Turkey was trying very hard to keep a hold on me and didn't want me to leave. It reminded me of the lyrics from the Eagle's hit song Hotel California; *'you can check out any time you like but you can never leave.'*

It's a cold but sunny morning and I am happily relaxing in the cozy warm kitchen of my friend's home in Spain and recalling the crazy chain of events that were blocking my departure from Turkey. It was a day of travel that I hope to never experience again.

The bus trip from Çanakkale to Istanbul went smoothly. It's always a long tedious six hour trip but I was used to it by now. When I eventually arrived in Istanbul, a friend met me at the bus station and took me and my luggage to my hotel in Ataköy. He dropped me off and returned to his work. Later that evening we would go out for dinner.

The first hiccup in my travel plans came when the hotel

receptionist greeted me with a nervous smile and declared that there was no electricity and that they didn't know when it would be back on. Hopefully, by 8 pm he had said. *Inshallah*!

It was February and it was freezing cold and snowy. No electricity meant no heating, no hot water for a shower and no internet. By booking.com standards this was a decent mid-range hotel with excellent reviews. It was just bad luck and I understood that it was out of their control but it was still difficult to deal with. The very apologetic receptionist softened the blow by bringing me candles, a coffee and a slice of cake. I tried to be positive and thought it was a good excuse to get under the blankets and have a nap for a few hours before we went out for dinner. Luckily when I returned from dinner, the electricity had been restored and my room was toasty warm.

At reservation through *booking.com* I had given my credit card details but messaged that I would pay in cash as I wanted to use up my Turkish liras. As it turned out, they took my cash as well as charging my credit card. Another inconvenience but luckily I was eventually refunded through *booking.com*.

I had booked a 6 am taxi to the airport for my early morning flight to Bilbao in Spain. By this stage I was just so happy to board the plane and finally let myself relax. After some light conversation with the man sitting next to me, I put in my earbuds and prepared to settle back and enjoy the next four hours. As my plane took off, I murmured my goodbyes to Istanbul and swore that I would return to visit friends and pick up some of my luggage that I had left behind. Of course, I knew that I would return one day as Turkey had been a big part of my life for over six years and I had made some wonderful friendships there. I could never have predicted just how soon my return would be.

With sweet music in my ears and letting go of all tensions, I started to doze off but was abruptly brought back to reality by my fellow passenger prodding my arm.

"What's up?" I said.

I wasn't too happy.

"We're going back," he said. "We're returning to Istanbul."

"What? Why?" I questioned.

And so after more than an hour into our flight, there had been a medical emergency and with no doctor on board, our plane was forced to return to Istanbul. Surely, this couldn't be happening. The pilot assured the passengers that he would fly as fast as he could. That was very reassuring.

We arrived back in Istanbul just after 11am and were met by two ambulances. Our plane had to refuel and then we had to wait our turn for the runway and after another two or more hours we once more took off and said goodbye to Istanbul, again. Goodbye Turkey!

Because of all the disruptions, the breakfast that we had missed turned into lunch and a glass of wine was most appreciated. There was quite a merry atmosphere on the plane now as we were finally on our way. I had left Turkey. I was looking forward to starting a new chapter of my life and teaching English in Spain. What more could go wrong now?

Due to the long delays with my flight, I had missed my connecting bus to Logroño and as the next bus wasn't for a few hours, I was faced with another dilemma. I didn't speak a single word of Spanish and so it wasn't easy finding out about other transport options. I went to the cafeteria at the bus station and was able to connect to the Wi-Fi. My friends had been expecting me and so I needed to communicate with them and tell them about my travel problems.

I was still a long way from my final destination and unfortunately more drama was ahead for me. The trip from Bilbao to Logroño would take an hour and a half by bus but much faster by car. My friends suggested a ride share website called Bla Bla Car and luckily there was a girl going my way within the hour. I contacted her and arranged for her to pick me up at the bus station. All was going well.

I had left my hotel at 6 am in the morning and it was now close to 6 pm. It was freezing and raining. Laura arrived at the bus station and we were on our way. In just over an hour I'd be sitting in front of the fire at my friend's home and relating the crazy events of the morning.

Wrong!

Laura and I hit it off immediately. She spoke English which was awesome. We had great conversation about life in the Basque country and La Rioja, life in Turkey, her studies and my plans. We planned to meet up for a beer in the coming days. Everything was going so well. We had about 80 kilometres left to go. We were travelling on the tollway which cost an exorbitant 14 euros. I mention the tollway because this is high quality road and supposedly safe from animals like deer and wild pigs, so where did this wild pig come from???

The wild pig ran into the front of our car, damaging the radiator. Plumes of smoke or steam arose from the front of the car and Laura slowly pulled in to the side of the road. We could see the dead pig behind us and the damage to the front of Laura's car. On the bright side, we were lucky that it hadn't been worse. Laura had handled the situation brilliantly.

It was -2 degrees and snowing as we waited on the side of the road for the police to arrive and make a report. Then we had to wait for the tow truck to tow us back to Bilbao and for the second time today, I was returning to where I had just come from. I was returning to Bilbao.

Eventually Laura's father came to take us both to Logroño and finally at around midnight I arrived at my friend's home.

What a day? It wasn't easy leaving Turkey.

Taking off my battle jacket

I'm taking off my battle jacket. I am slowly peeling away the layers of defence. Day by day, I can feel myself relaxing and releasing all the inner tension that I had been holding on to.

For the last six years, I had been living in Turkey. The last five of those years in Çanakkale, a medium sized town in northwest Turkey. In 2008, when I first moved to Izmit to start teaching English, I was fresh. I was enthusiastic. I was very trusting, probably a bit naive and definitely a lot more accepting. I was in Turkey. Just the name 'Istanbul' excited me and the idea of living in Turkey was a dream come true. I had always loved travel. In my early twenties, I had lived in London, Jersey and Italy. I enjoyed experiencing new cultures and Turkey was exotic, colourful and exciting.

That first year in Turkey was wonderful. I knew that I wanted to stay longer. I had travelled around Turkey with my son and just fell in love with the country. There were incidents that weren't so great but they added to the adventure and....... I was just more resilient or more accepting.

As I said, I was trusting, so when I got my first flat in Izmit, and my school suggested I open my gas account in a student's name as I didn't yet have my Residency Permit, I thought that was a kind offer. I didn't expect that when I wanted to leave and close the account, this student couldn't be contacted or found by the school or myself, meaning that he would collect my rather large deposit. Ok, no big deal. I moved on.

Unwanted advances by much younger men simply amused me. Being cheated in stores annoyed me, but again I just let it go. Once in Goreme, with my son, we wanted to buy a bus ticket to Kayseri but the ticket sales man insisted he could sell us a cheaper ticket all the way to Şanlıurfa. We insisted on just a ticket to Kayseri and we would purchase the second ticket in Kayseri. He was enraged and told us we can't take the bus as it was full.

When the bus pulled in it was far from full and after asking the driver we were given the permission to board. As we were storing our luggage under the bus, the enraged ticket salesman flew down to the bus and grabbed my son by his arm. He proceeded to pull our packs off the bus. It was high drama that attracted quite a crowd of onlookers and many came to our rescue. As we eventually boarded the bus, we were cheered on by the other passengers and bystanders and the ticket vendor was shamed. This is just one of many crazy incidents…many incidents where my personal space was violated… where I was harassed and even experienced what would be considered assault in my country……….but I just moved on and they were just colourful memories….another day in Turkey……part of the great adventure……I thought.

I realize now that I was slowly but surely building up walls of defence, layers of distrust and suspicion. I was getting used to putting on my battle jacket and preparing for the worst. By 2014, I realized that I had become hardened; I scared myself when I reacted aggressively to the unwanted advances of men or the overcharging by a taxi driver in Istanbul or the pushing in line at the post office. I realized that I had lost all trust, and I always expected the worst....and sadly most of time I was right. I knew it was time to move on. I felt that I had reached my breaking point and I needed to muster the energy to leave my home and leave Turkey.

I relocated to Spain. It was a big decision and a big move but I knew I had to do it. It was over the first few weeks that I came to notice how often I was pleasantly surprised. When I had expected problems due to my Turkish conditioning, they just didn't happen. I prepared for the usual battles but there were no battles. For example; I visited an agency to find a flat. I was expecting to be lied to, cheated, to be charged a hefty agent's fee......I was now conditioned this way but none of those things happened! I simple signed a lease and paid a month's rent in advance and moved in.

Now, this is a furnished flat and guess what; it's really furnished and has everything. When I rented a 'furnished flat' in Çanakkale, the kitchen was bare and the blinds that we saw only came to half way, which meant I was fully exposed and needed to buy curtains. When I asked the agent about full length blinds, I was told that it's my bad luck and I should have noticed the blinds before I moved in. This furnished flat had been falsely represented by the agent. She told me if I didn't like it I could move, which I did a couple weeks later....and naturally I lost my hefty agent's fee and deposit as well as being charged her estimated fee for water, electric and gas.

My new flat in Spain had a little electricity problem. Again I expected the worst. But no! My landlord didn't expect me to pay for the electrician and he didn't try to kiss me or be in any way suggestive, and he was simply apologetic about the inconvenience. Wow...I was realizing more and more just how much I had become conditioned to always expect a battle. Being a solo woman in Turkey isn't easy.

Another example; I took a taxi and again as a foreigner I was expecting the worst.

"How much?" I asked.

The meter read five euros.

"Five euros," said the taxi driver.

What? Can it be true?

Every day I was more and more delighted by this sense of honesty and every day I was feeling my suspicions and distrust slowly but surely dissolving away.

I know this all sounds negative about Turkey and I do still love Turkey and will still holiday there and visit friends but visiting Turkey and living in Turkey are two completely different experiences. For a solo woman living in Turkey, you need to be tough, vigilant, and always on guard. It can be very difficult and at times frustrating, exhausting and exasperating.

On the bright side, I survived and fortunately there was no major damage. I can still look back at all the wonderful times. I know of many solo expat women who have lost small fortunes to unscrupulous Turkish con men either in business dealings or through bogus relationships. Actually, even a female Turkish professor friend of mine lost thousands of liras by feeling obliged and bullied into signing the documents and paying a deposit for a property that didn't even exist. Yes, living in Turkey isn't easy for anyone, but for women, Turkish and foreign, the challenges are so much greater.

TURKISH DIARIES

Glossary

anne — *mother*

ayip sana — *shame on you*

ayran — *a cold and refreshing yoghurt based drink*

baklava — *pastry made with sheets of filo, nuts and honey*

banyo — *bathroom or bath*

büyükanne — *grandmother*

buyrun — *come in, what can I do for you?*

çiğ köfte — *a raw meatball dish, also common with bulgur*

dondurma — *ice cream*

durmak — *stop*

emlak — *real estate agent*

fez — *a red felt hat worn in the Ottoman days*

garson — *waiter*

hamam — *Turkish bath*

havlu — *towel*

hoca — *teacher*

hoşbulduk — *I'm honoured to be here*

hoşgeldiniz — *welcome*

incir — *fig*

köfte — *meatballs*

kordon — *promenade, sea front*

kunefe — *sweet, syrupy, semolina style dessert*

lokum — *Turkish delight*

lütfen — *please*

manti — *a Turkish dumpling filled with meat and spices*

memnun oldum—*pleased to meet you*

merhaba — *hello*

peştamal — *towel used in the hamam*

salep — *flour from an orchid root, a drink made with hot milk*

seks — *sex*

tamam — *okay*

teşekkür ederim — *thank you*

yabanci — *foreigner*

A TURKISH AFFAIR

On the brink of divorce, and with her fiftieth birthday just around the corner, Zoe's life is far from perfect. Out of the blue, she receives a card from an ex-lover from over twenty six years ago which completely turns her world upside down and has her questioning her life. She reminisces on how they first met in 1980 when she was backpacking through Greece and struggles with her decision to be reunited with him again in Turkey in 2007. Together they travel to Cappadocia for a six day sojourn and to see if there could possibly be any future in their relationship.

A Turkish Affair is also available on Amazon in either e-book or paperback format.

TURKISH DIARIES

ABOUT THE AUTHOR

Matilda was born in England but lived most of her life in Australia. After her divorce she craved adventure and looked to find a means of financing her travels. English teaching was the ticket and she subsequently moved to Turkey to begin her new career at a language academy near Istanbul.

Having lived in Turkey for over 6 years and experienced the vivid colour and culture, she was inspired to write and in 2016 she self-published her first book, *A Turkish Affair.*

With the changing social and political climate in Turkey, Matilda felt it was time to move on and in 2015 she relocated to northern Spain but she still reminisces about those memorable years spent in Turkey.

Every day of living in Turkey was an adventure and Matilda draws her inspiration from those years.

Matilda can be contacted here: matildavoss@gmail.com

THANK YOU

If you're reading this, then you must have bought the print version of *Turkish Diaries* and for that I am very grateful. I would also be really happy if you could leave a review on Amazon.

If you enjoyed *Turkish Diaries,* please check out *A Turkish Affair* also available for download or in paperback format.

Keep in touch as I have more stories coming soon. You can follow my author's page for alerts when my next book will be released.

Thank you so much for your support.

Best wishes always,

Matilda

TURKISH DIARIES

Printed in Great Britain
by Amazon

22227240R00142